The North West Highlands and Skye

by
F. R. BANKS

Letts Motor Tour Guides

Printed and Published by
Charles Letts & Company Limited
London, Edinburgh & New York
Head Office:
Diary House, Borough Road, London, S.E.1

Publishing Consultant: Lionel Leventhal

Cover Artist: Kenneth Farnhill

Maps: Alan Walton

The North-West Highlands and Skye
by F. R. Banks
first published 1969
© Charles Letts & Company Limited, 1969

12   LSC

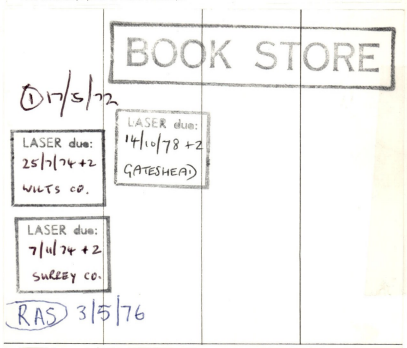

How to use your
Letts Motor Tour Guide

The best way to see Britain is, for most people, by car. This Tour Guide has been specially designed to lead you—the motorist—to all that is best in its chosen area.

The North-West Highlands, with Mull, Skye and the Outer Hebrides

This series of tours covers the whole of the Highlands of Scotland north-west of the road through the Great Glen from Fort William to Inverness, along the line of which it links up with those in the Letts Motor Tour Guide to *The Highlands from Edinburgh to Inverness*. The tours take in also the islands of Mull and Skye and the Outer Hebridean islands which are connected with the mainland and with each other by car ferries.

One of the most fascinating regions of Britain, this is also one of the most remote and least spoiled. It has a wealth of striking mountains, lovely glens, rugged coasts and delightful islands, beautiful fjords and inland lochs, charming old towns and villages, interesting castles and unusual prehistoric remains.

The Tours

There are ten motor tours in this guide and each tour covers between 100 and 200 miles, so that a single tour will provide two or more good days' motoring. All the tours are circular, and so you can start and finish a route at any point you may choose. The book is yours to use in your own way.

Car Ferries

Ferry steamers with drive-on/drive-off facilities for cars ply between Oban, Craignure (on the island of Mull) and Lochaline, between Mallaig and Armadale (on Skye), between Mallaig and Lochboisdale (in the Outer Hebrides), and between Uig (Skye), Lochmaddy and Tarbert (Outer Hebrides). The services, however, are infrequent and operate only on weekdays (*not Sundays*), and advance reservation is advisable, especially in the height of summer. Information regarding times, fares and booking may be obtained from the head office of David MacBrayne, Ltd., 44 Robertson Street, Glasgow, C.2. The car ferry service from Kyle of Lochalsh to Kyleakin (Skye) operates daily (including Sundays) at frequent intervals, and no reservations are accepted. The ferries across Loch Carron at Strome and across Loch Cairnbawn at Kylesku carry a limited number of cars, and though services are frequent a long wait can often be expected in summer (as much as 2 hours in the height of the season). The Strome Ferry operates only on weekdays (not on Sundays), and the Kylesku Ferry does not operate during bad weather. No reservations may be made on these ferries.

The Maps

The maps (one for each tour and a larger one for the whole area) have been specially designed to show clearly all the information you will need—without being unduly technical. Readers who lack expertise in map-reading will have no difficulty in following the directions and the route. The main approach roads to the tours are also indicated.

Reference Books

For those who wish to use more detailed maps, Sheets 2, 3 and 4 of the Ordnance Survey quarter-inch maps cover most of the area. Particulars are given in the tours of the days and times of opening for houses, castles and museums, and these are correct at the time of going to press. The most recent information can be obtained from *Historic Houses, Castles and Gardens in Great Britain,* which is published annually in February. Details regarding museums and art galleries are given in *Museums and Galleries in Great Britain,* published yearly in July.

Particulars of hotels, restaurants and inns are given in the annual reference guide, *Hotels and Restaurants in Britain,* published by the British Travel Association, and in *Where to Stay,* published by the Highlands and Islands Development Board and obtainable from them or from the Scottish Tourist Board (2 Rutland Place, Edinburgh 1), from whom also other information may be obtained. Places where accommodation is available are indicated in the tours. An annual selective and critical guide to eating places is Raymond Postgate's *Good Food Guide,* and a more extensive annual critical guide to hotels, restaurants, pubs and inns is written by Egon Ronay.

This Series

This Motor Tour Guide is part of a continuing series which will cover the whole of the British Isles. (A list of other titles can be found on the back cover.) Every effort has been made to ensure the accuracy at the time of going to press of all factual information, but some of this is of the kind which may change from year to year. The publishers would therefore be grateful if readers would draw their attention to any improvements which may be made to these Motor Tour Guides. In this way, future editions can be made as complete and useful as possible.

Contents

Maps

Tour Maps are on the first or second page of each tour.

Port of
Ness

A857

Lewis

Stornoway

A858

A859

Steamer

Harris

Tarbert

Car Ferries

North Uist
A865

Lochmaddy

Uig

A856

Benbecula

Dunvegan
A850
Portree

A865

Kyle of
Lochal

South Uist
A863

Lochboisdale

Sligachan

A850
Broadford (4)

Barra

Car Ferry

Kylea

Castlebay

A851

Armadale

Ca
Fe

Steamer

Mallaig (5)

A8

A8

Strontian

A884
Lochaline

Tobermory

A848

C
Fe

Craignure

Iona

A849

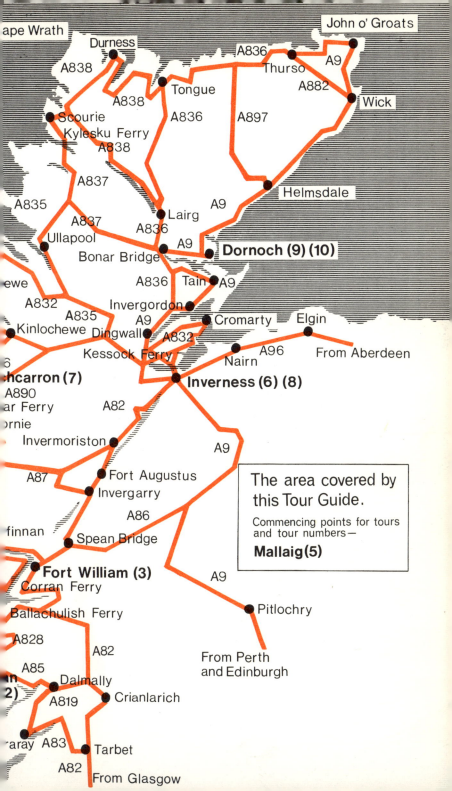

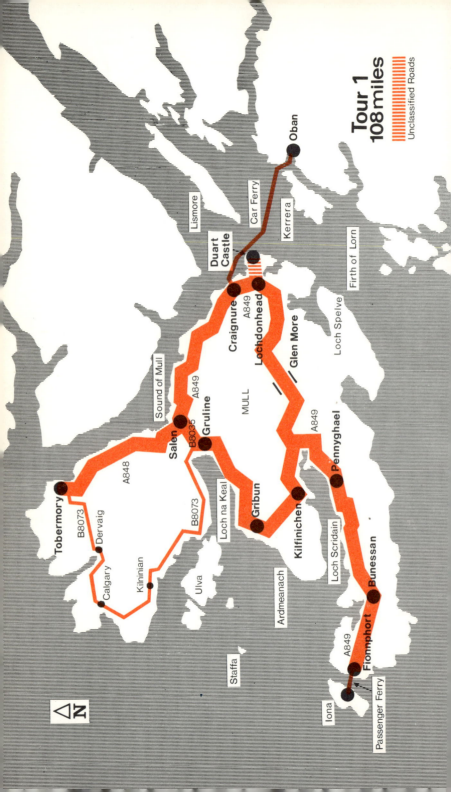

Tour 1
108 miles

Unclassified Roads

Oban

Lismore

Car Ferry

Kerrera

Firth of Lorn

Duart Castle

Craignure

A849

Lochdonhead

Glen More

Loch Spelve

Sound of Mull

A849

Gruline

B8035

Salen

MULL

A849

Pennyghael

Loch na Keal

Gribun

Kilfinichen

A848

Tobermory

B8073

Dervaig

B8073

Kilninian

Ulva

Ardmeanach

Loch Scridain

Bunessan

Calgary

Staffa

A849

Fionnphort

Iona

Passenger Ferry

N

1. Round the Island of Mull

This tour explores Mull, one of the Inner Hebrides, a mountainous and rugged island separated from the mainland by the Firth of Lorn or Lorne, the seaward approach to the long Loch Linnhe, and from the peninsula of Morvern by the Sound of Mull. The island is roughly triangular in shape and about 30 miles in length, but its irregular and rocky coast-line conceals numerous sea-lochs and sandy bays. The broad fjord of Loch na Keal, the head of which is less than 3 miles from Salen, on the Sound of Mull, almost cuts the island into two. The southern half of Mull is dominated by the great mountain mass culminating in Ben More, the highest peak, rising between Loch na Keal and Loch Scridain, to the south of which is the Ross of Mull, a long promontory of granite extending west to end opposite the small island of Iona, the cradle of Christianity in Britain and the burial-place of the early Scottish kings. The only town on Mull is Tobermory, near the northern end. The scenery of the island, though stern and wild, has a distinctive charm of its own. It is noted for its sunsets and for its mild and sometimes damp climate; Dr Johnson, here during a rainy spell in 1773, thought it was 'worse than Skye'. David Balfour, in Stevenson's *Kidnapped,* found his way with difficulty from Erraid, an island off the south-west end, to the coast opposite Lochaline, in Morvern. The roads on Mull are invariably narrow and winding, requiring care, though passing places have been provided on the A roads, as on all roads of this class in the North-West Highlands. A Car Ferry service operates on weekdays from Oban, on the mainland, to Craignure (taking $\frac{3}{4}$ hour), going on thence to Lochaline, in Morvern (Tour 2). Steamers ply round the island in summer, calling at Iona and Staffa (weather permitting) and at Tobermory.

Oban (numerous hotels) is a thriving fishing port and market town, and a popular holiday and yachting resort, on the shores and slopes of a sheltered bay, almost landlocked by the island of Kerrera and renowned for its views across the Firth of Lorn to the mountains of Mull (best at sunset). Its growth coincided with the development of the tourist industry in the Western Highlands in the 19th century, and the town in consequence is mainly of modern aspect. The Railway Quay, on the south side of Oban Bay, is usually busy with steamers and fishing boats. From the North Pier, overlooking the Inner Harbour, the bay is skirted by the Corran Esplanade (with a concert pavilion), leading to the distinctive white Christ Church (1957) and the granite Roman Catholic Cathedral (by Sir Giles G. Scott, 1932) of the diocese of Argyll and the Isles. Farther on is the ruined medieval tower of Dunollie Castle, the stronghold of the MacDougalls, Lords of Lorn, and the shore road ends at Ganavan, a favourite bathing-place on a fine sandy bay. On the hill behind the town is the prominent but unfinished McCaig Tower, a circular structure begun about 1890, commanding a wonderful view over the firth to Mull and the hills of Morvern. The Argyllshire Highland Gathering, a colourful occasion, with games, piping, dancing, etc., takes place annually in September.

The car ferry, starting from the North Pier, rounds the north end of Kerrera and crosses the Firth of Lorn, opening up a magnificent view to the north and east of successive mountain ranges from Ben Nevis to Ben Cruachan. Ahead rise the mountainous profile of Mull and the steep face of Morvern. In the mouth of Loch Linnhe, to the right, is the flat and narrow island of Lismore. Opposite the lighthouse at the south end, marked by a beacon but visible only at low water, is the Lady Rock, on which one of the Macleans of Duart marooned his wife, only to have her rescued by fishermen. The ferry passes Duart Point, with its castle, and skirts the shore of Mull to Craignure.

Craignure is a small village with a steamer pier, below the mountain of Dùn da Ghaoithe (2512 feet), at the entrance to the Sound of Mull, a strait about 2 miles wide separating the mountainous Mull from the high cliffs of Morvern.

A849 south from Craignure, passing the 19th-century Torosay Castle (1 mile), beyond which a by-road on the left leads to Duart Castle (2 miles more).

Duart Castle (admission May to September, Monday-Friday, 10.30 to 6; July and August, Sundays also, 2.30 to 6), finely situated on a headland enclosing a sandy bay, is the ancient seat of the chief of the Clan Maclean. Built about 1250 and extended in 1633, it was ruined in 1691, but was repurchased by the Macleans in 1911 and has been well restored. The 26th chief died here in 1937 at the age of 101; the present chief, Sir Charles Maclean, is the Chief Scout of the Commonwealth. To the south on the shore, which affords a fine view up Loch Linnhe to the mountains of Appin and Ben Nevis, is a lighthouse in memory of William Black (died 1898), many of whose novels are set in the Western Highlands and Islands.

A849 on to Lochdonhead (2 miles from Craignure), at the head of a sandy creek, and thence past the north end of Loch Spelve to Strathcoil (3½ miles farther).

Loch Spelve is an irregularly shaped loch with a very narrow entrance from the Firth of Lorn. A hilly by-road on the left from Strathcoil skirts the west shore of the loch, below Creach Beinn (2289 feet), and goes on past Loch Uisg to the head of the broad Loch Buie (7½ miles). On the shore here are the ruins of Moy Castle, once a stronghold of the Maclaines of Lochbuie, and the house where Johnson and Boswell stayed on their Highland tour; and to the north is a stone circle.

A849 on through the wild and lonely Glen More (see below) descending the Coladoir River to the head of Loch Scridain (10 miles).

Loch Scridain is a long inlet of the sea separating the peninsula of Ardmeanach, on the north, from the Ross of Mull. To the north of its head rises the graceful peak of Ben More (3169 feet). the highest mountain in Mull, the end of a long range that extends east to Beinn Talaidh or Talla (2496 feet), a pointed peak well seen from Glen More. B8035, rounding the north shore of the loch (see below), is the direct road to Tobermory.

A849 on along the south shore of Loch Scridain to Pennyghael (3 miles).

Pennyghael is on the Ross of Mull, a long peninsula, mainly of granite and remarkable for its quarries and the scenery of its southern shore, where the cliffs, rising to over 1000 feet and among the highest in Scotland, are capped with outcrops of basalt. There is no road along this shore, but a by-road runs south from Pennyghael through Glen Leidle to Carsaig (3½ miles), a scattered village of neat cottages and a prominent church. To the west, a waterfall descends the steep fissured cliffs of Aoineadh Mòr, and in Malcolm's Point, farther west, are caves and tunnels forced by the sea through the basaltic rock.

A849 on along the southern shore of Loch Scridain, opposite the hilly promontory of Ardmeanach, to Bunessan (10 miles; hotel), a village on Loch na Lathaich, and thence to Fionnphort (6 miles; small hotel), for the passenger ferry to Iona.

Iona (hotels), the birthplace of Christianity in Britain, is a treeless island 3½ miles long, separated from Mull by the Sound of Iona, a strait only about 1 mile wide. It was here, in the 6th century, that St. Columba, voyaging from Ireland, founded the famous monastery that became the burial-place of Scottish kings and chiefs, and from here he set out on his journeys to convert Scotland to Christianity. The monastery was destroyed in the early 9th century by Norwegian pirates, but a new abbey, for Benedictines, was founded in 1203, and this served as the cathedral of the see of Sodor (i.e. the Hebrides) from 1499 until the dissolution in 1578, after which it was annexed to the Protestant bishopric of the Isles. To the west of the village, which is grouped round the ferry landing, are the early-13th-century ruins of the small priory church of an Augustinian nunnery. A lane from this, passing the tall 15th-century Maclean's Cross, leads to St. Oran's Cemetery, the oldest Christian burial-ground in Scotland, with the graves of many kings and chiefs, down to King Duncan, who died in 1040, murdered, according to Shakespeare, by Macbeth. In the cemetery is the small St. Oran's Chapel, said to have been built by Queen Margaret in 1080, and containing the tomb of the 'Lord of the Isles' of Sir Walter Scott's

11

poem. Opposite the west front is the high 10th-century St. Martin's Cross, carved with Runic ornament and figures. Beyond is the Cathedral, originally the abbey church, but mainly of the 16th century and often altered since, with a square tower above the crossing, notable carved capitals in the choir, and a rich sacristy doorway of about 1500. Together with the neighbouring monastic buildings, it has been restored by the Iona Community, a religious brotherhood founded in 1938 by Dr George (now Lord) Macleod. From the higher parts of the island a wide panorama opens, extending south to the islands of Colonsay, Jura and Islay, and in clear weather the hills of Ireland are visible. To the north is Staffa, a small uninhabited island famous for its beautiful caves, with their fascinating basaltic rock formations.

A849 back from Fionnphort to the head of Loch Scridain (19 miles), then B8035, rounding the north shore of the loch, to Kilfinichen Church (4 miles).

Kilfinichen Church stands on a small bay opening from the loch, with the noble peak of Ben More rising to the north-east. The by-road going on along the shore leads to Burg, an experimental farm of 2000 acres belonging to the National Trust for Scotland, on the peninsula of Ardmeanach, noted for its cliffs and caves.

B8035, ascending Glen Seilisdeir and crossing the neck of Ardmeanach, to Gribun (5 miles).

Gribun is on the south shore of the large Loch na Keal, which is bounded here by the Gribun Rocks, an imposing range of over-hanging cliffs. Offshore is the green island of Inch Kenneth, where Johnson and Boswell were entertained by Sir Alan Maclean, and farther out is the hilly island of Ulva, with Staffa away to the west.

B8035 along the shore of Loch na Keal, below the northern slopes of Ben More, to Gruline (9 miles).

Gruline, with its church, lies near the broad head of Loch na Keal, the 'Loch Gyle' of Thomas Campbell's ballad, 'Lord Ullin's Daughter'. Tobermory (see below) may be reached from here by B8073, a narrow, twisting and very hilly road round the north-west arm of Mull. It skirts the north shore of Loch na Keal, passes the road (7 miles) leading to the passenger ferry for Ulva, with its basaltic cliffs and caves, and runs alongside Loch Tuath, where it passes Kilninian (6 miles), which has carved Celtic stones in the churchyard. It then crosses open moorland to Calgary ($6\frac{1}{2}$ miles), on a fine sandy bay, from which Calgary in Alberta was named. To the west, out to sea, are seen the long low islands of Tiree and Coll. The road turns east, touching the head of the narrow Loch Cuan at Dervaig ($4\frac{1}{2}$ miles; hotel at the Mull Little Theatre), then ascends to pass the Mishnish Lochs for Tobermory (8 miles more).

12

B8035 on from Gruline, across a wooded strath, the narrowest part of Mull, to Salen (2½ miles).

Salen (hotels) is a village on a bay facing across the beautiful Sound of Mull to the mountains of Morvern. On a rocky promontory above the mouth of the Aros, north of the bay, are the ruins of Aros Castle, once a stronghold of the Macdonalds, Lords of the Isles.

A848 north, passing near Aros Castle, and on above the Sound of Mull to Tobermory (10 miles).

Tobermory (hotels), the 'well of St. Mary', founded in 1788 as a herring-fishing port, is now a favourite summer resort and the chief place on Mull. It is delightfully placed on the shore and above the slopes of a secluded bay sheltered by thick woods, with attractive houses facing the quay and the steamer pier. To the south of the bay, which is almost landlocked by the low island of Calve, are charming waterfalls in the beautiful wooded grounds of Aros House. A Spanish galleon, supposedly laden with treasure, was wrecked in the bay in 1588, after being blown up by Donald Glas Maclean, a hostage who found access to the powder magazine. Attempts to raise treasure have been made since the 17th century, but nothing of value has yet been found. The Mull Highland Games, a popular occasion, are held in Erray Park each year in July. From the heights above the town there are splendid views across the Sound and the mouth of Loch Sunart to the hills and cliffs of Ardnamurchan.

A848 back to Salen (10 miles), then A849 on along the Sound of Mull, with fine views of the Morvern shore, the narrow entrance to Loch Aline and the ruins of Ardtornish Castle, to Craignure (11½ miles), for the car ferry to Oban or to Lochaline (see Tour 2).

Tour 2
120 miles

N

A82 From Inverness

Fort William

A830

Loch Eil

A82

Car Ferry

Ballachulish Ferry

Kinlocheil

Camusnagaul

Glenfinnan

A830

A861

Ardgour

Corran

Inversanda

A861

Camasnacroise

A830

Lochailort

Loch Eilt

Loch Shiel

Strontian

B8043

Loch Linnhe

A85 From Glasgow and Edinburgh

Oban

A861

A861

Kinlochmoidart

Sunart

A861

B8043

Glen Geal

Lismore

Car Ferries

Sound of Arisaig

Acharacle

Salen

Loch Sunart

A884

A884

Larachbeg

A884

Craignure

Car Ferries

Morvern

Lochaline

Sound of Mull

Mull

Ardnamurchan

2. Between Loch Linnhe and the Atlantic Coast

This tour explores the broad rugged peninsula, from 22 to 28 miles wide, extending between the great inlet of Loch Linnhe and the open waters of the Atlantic. It is a little-visited region, with lonely mountain ranges divided from each other by long and beautiful lochs. The peninsula comprises the districts of Morvern (or Morven), on the south, towards the Sound of Mull, which separates it from that island; Ardnamurchan and Moidart, on the west, bounded by the open sea; Sunart, in the centre, between Loch Sunart and Loch Shiel; and Ardgour and Kingairloch on the east, facing Loch Linnhe and the mountains of Appin and Ben Nevis. The roads of this area are mostly winding and narrow (though with passing places), except for the fine new road between Kinlochmoidart and Lochailort and the more-frequented road (part of the 'Road to the Isles'; see Tour 3) between Lochailort and Glenfinnan. A Car Ferry service operates on weekdays from Oban to Lochaline (taking about 1½ hours), and a small ferry (with room for 4 to 5 cars), running daily, connects Corran, in Ardgour, with the Fort William-Ballachulish road.

Oban and the car ferry route thence to Craignure, on Mull, are described in Tour 1 (pages 9-10).

Beyond Craignure the ferry enters the Sound of Mull and crosses to the Morvern coast, passing near Ardtornish Castle (see below) before reaching Lochaline.

Lochaline is a modern village at the narrow entrance to the enchanting loch of the same name. The inhabitants (about 35) of the outlying islands of St. Kilda were moved bodily to this region in 1930. Ardtornish Castle stands on a bold point above the sea, backed by cliffs over which fall two graceful cascades. The unimpressive ruins, with a square keep, are those of a 14th-century stronghold of the Macdonalds, 'Lords of the Isles', described in Sir Walter Scott's epic poem, though at the date of the poem's setting their headquarters were in Islay. Near the church of Lochaline, at Keil, are early carved slabs portraying the kilt. B849 runs west along the north shore of the beautiful Sound of Mull, passing the white house of Fiunary, the home of Norman Macleod (died 1862), the author, and ending at Drimnin (10½ miles), with fine views of the north wing of Mull and the peninsula of Ardnamurchan.

A884 from Lochaline, skirting the loch shore to **Larachbeg** (3 miles).

Larachbeg is a hamlet in the wooded glen between Loch Arienas and Loch Aline, at the head of which is the turreted 15th-century Kinlochaline Castle.

A884 on through the glen, then up the wild Glen Geal, climbing over towards Glen Dubh, at the head of which (8½ miles) the return route via Camasnacroise comes in. A884 on, crossing a steep ridge to the south shore of Loch Sunart, then east round the head of the loch (7 miles) and by A861 (left) to Strontian (1½ miles).

Strontian (hotels) is a village delightfully situated near the east end of the beautiful serpent-like Loch Sunart, an arm of the sea over 20 miles long, separating Morvern, on the south, from Sunart and Ardnamurchan. In the glen of the Strontian River, to the north, are the lead mines (now disused) where the element strontium was discovered. To the north-west rises the distinctive peak of Beinn Resipol (2775 feet).

A861 on, along the north shore of Loch Sunart, to Salen (10 miles).

Salen (hotel) is a village and angling resort on a small bay of the wooded shore of the loch. B8007, an inferior road with few passing places, goes on west near the loch to Glenborrodale (7½ miles) then winds away inland to avoid the rugged Ben Hiant (1729 feet), before returning towards the sea again at Kilchoan (12 miles; hotels), a village facing the junction of Loch Sunart with the Sound of Mull. On the shore to the south-east here are the fine ruins of Mingary Castle, a stronghold of the MacIans, a younger branch of the Macdonalds, and described by Scott in *The Lord of the Isles*. James IV held court here in 1495 to receive the submission of the chieftains of the isles; and in 1644 it was taken by Alastair Macdonald for the Marquess of Montrose. To the west of Kilchoan Bay are some of the fine riven cliffs of Ardnamurchan. B8007 goes on across the peninsula to Achosnich (4 miles), near the white sand-dunes of Sanna Bay, while a rough by-road leads to Ardnamurchan Point, where a lighthouse marks the westernmost point of the Scottish mainland. The wide seaward view includes the islands of Coll and Tiree, to the west, and those of Muick and Rhum, to the north, with the mountains of Skye beyond.

A861 north from Salen, crossing the isthmus between Loch Sunart and Loch Shiel, to Acharacle (2½ miles).

Acharacle (hotels) is an angling resort near the foot of Loch Shiel, up which a steamer plies to Glenfinnan (see below; page 17). B8044 runs west from the village across Kentra Moss to Ardtoe (3½ miles), on the sandy inlet of Kentra Bay, while an unclassified road, leaving A861 north of Shiel Bridge, follows the river downstream to its mouth in Loch Moidart near Dorlin. Offshore here, but reached on foot except at high tides, is Castle Tirrim or Tioram, a ruined 14th-century stronghold of the Macdonalds of Clanranald, burned during the Jacobite Rising in 1715.

A861, crossing the Shiel River (see above), then east, passing a by-road to Dalelia, a small angling place on Loch Shiel at which the steamer calls; then north, across the ridge between the loch and Glen Moidart, with splendid views, to Kinlochmoidart (7½ miles).

Kinlochmoidart, or Ardmolich, is at the head of Loch Moidart, a lovely sea-loch with finely wooded shores, penetrating into the lonely district of Moidart. Prince Charles Edward Stewart stayed with the Macdonalds here before the raising of the clans at Glenfinnan in 1745, and seven beeches commemorate the 'Seven Men of Moidart' who were his first supporters. The steep hills to the north of Glen Moidart culminate in Rois Bheinn (2895 feet).

A861, a newly-constructed road, west along the north shore of Loch Moidart, then north over a ridge to Glenuig Bay, on the south shore of the Sound of Arisaig, with a fine view of Eigg; then east along the shore of the beautiful Loch Ailort, under the northern flanks of Rois Bheinn, to Lochailort (13 miles), at the head of the loch.

Lochailort is described in Tour 3 (page 22).

A830 east past Loch Eilt to Glenfinnan (9½ miles) and thence to the head of Loch Eil (4½ miles).

Glenfinnan, Loch Eilt and Loch Eil are described in Tour 3 (pages 21-22).

A861 (right) along the south shore of Loch Eil to Camusnagaul (10½ miles).

Camusnagaul lies in an angle of Loch Linnhe, a little below the place where it is entered by the strait issuing from Loch Eil. It faces across the upper end of the loch to Fort William (Tour 3), which can be reached by passenger ferry. Beyond the loch rises the massive bulk of Ben Nevis, dominating the surrounding country of Lochaber.

A861 south along the shore of Loch Linnhe, below the slopes of Stob Coire a' Chearcaill (2525 feet) and Sgurr na h-Eanchainne (2395 feet), heights of the district of Ardgour, to Corran (11½ miles).

Corran (hotel), or Ardgour, is a village on the west side of the Corran Narrows, which divide Loch Linnhe into a narrow upper reach, extending to Fort William, and a much wider lower section, reaching to the Firth of Lorn. A car ferry crosses the Narrows to reach the road from Fort William to North Ballachulish, which is on Loch Leven, a sea-loch that enters Loch Linnhe a little south of the Narrows (see Letts Motor Tour Guide to *The Highlands from Edinburgh to Inverness*).

A861 on across the foot of Glen Gour and thence by the loch shore to Inversanda (6½ miles).

Inversanda is on a small bay of the broad Loch Linnhe, facing across to the mouth of Loch Leven and the rugged mountains of Appin, the country of the Stewarts. A861, an indifferent road, turns inland through Glen Tarbert, beneath the flanks of the fine peak of Garbh Bheinn (2903 feet), noted for its rock scenery, to the head of Loch Sunart and Strontian (8 miles; see above).

B8043, a narrow road branching left from A861 and returning to the shore of Loch Linnhe at Cilmalieu (4 miles), and thence to Camasnacroise (3½ miles).

Camasnacroise is situated on a small bay of Loch Linnhe, at the foot of Glenalmadale, the head of which is overlooked by the fine peak of Creach Bheinn (2800 feet). The wide view over the loch includes the mountains of Appin and the long green island of Lismore.

B8043 on, skirting Loch a' Choire, an inlet of Loch Linnhe, and ascending through the wild district of Kingairloch, passing the smaller Loch Uisge before reaching the junction with A884 in 6 miles (see page 16). A884 (left), descending to Lochaline (11½ miles farther), for the car ferry to Craignure and Oban.

3. The Roads to the Isles

This tour goes out and returns by two of the roads to Skye, the largest of the Inner Hebrides, a wild and lonely island remarkable for the beauty of its coast and mountain scenery and for its mild and often misty climate. Starting from the favourite tourist resort of Fort William, with its thriving new industries, the route takes the famous 'Road to the Isles' via Glenfinnan, where Prince Charles Edward Stewart raised his standard at the outset of the Jacobite Rising of 1745. The road ends at the fishing port of Mallaig, which is connected by a Car Ferry (on weekdays only), taking ½ hour, with Armadale, on Skye. At Broadford, the route links up with that of Tour 4, which takes in the major part of the island. The return to the mainland is made by the small and busy Car Ferry (no reservations) between Kyleakin and Kyle of Lochalsh, from which Fort William is reached by the beautiful road skirting Loch Alsh and Loch Duich and then traversing Glen Shiel to the Great Glen, which runs right across country from Inverness to Fort William and divides the Northern and Western Highlands from the Central Highlands. Some of the roads on this tour are still narrow and winding, though in other places motoring has been made easier by new or improved stretches of road.

Fort William (numerous hotels), near the head of Loch Linnhe, where it turns west towards Loch Eil, is a busy town and a popular tourist and sailing centre, the usual starting point for the ascent of Ben Nevis. The 17th-century fort, rebuilt for William III (after whom it was named) with the object of quelling the rebellious Highlanders, was pulled down in 1890 to make way for the West Highland Railway. The town, mostly developed since the opening of the railway in 1894, has been given a new lease of life by the large industries established in the neighbourhood. In Cameron Square is the interesting West Highland Museum (admission weekdays, 9.30 to 5, June-August to 9), containing old 'bygones', farm implements and domestic utensils, collections illustrating local geology and industry and tartan weaving, and Jacobite relics. Cow Hill, to the south-east of the town, affords a fine view of the beautiful Glen Nevis, with the slopes of Ben Nevis (4418 feet), the highest mountain in Britain, rising above it.

A82 northward from High Street to Inverlochy (1½ miles).

Inverlochy, at the mouth of the Lochy in Loch Linnhe, and now practically a suburb of Fort William, has huge aluminium works, connected with Loch Treig, 15 miles away to the east, by a pipeline through Ben Nevis. The ruined old Inverlochy Castle is a large square fortress, probably of the late 15th century. The 19th-century Castle, over a mile farther on, near the Spean Bridge road (see page 25), is now the centre of an extensive cattle ranch.

A830 (left), crossing the Lochy to Banavie (1½ miles).

19

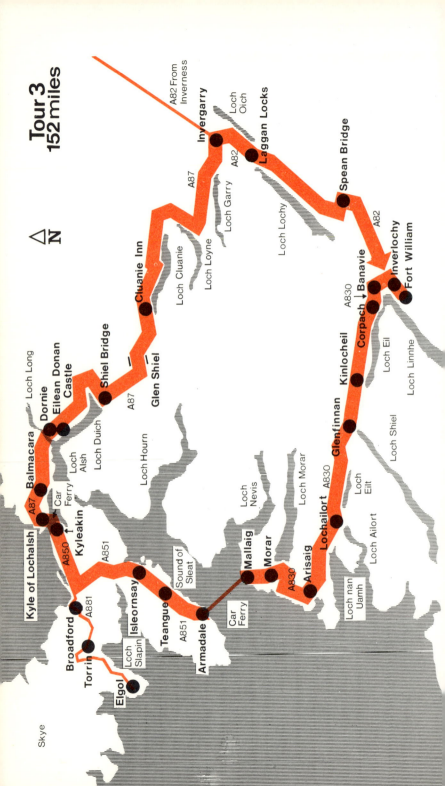

Banavie (hotels) is a village on the Caledonian Canal, a master-piece of engineering which was opened in 1822 and enlarged in 1847. It traverses the Great Glen between Loch Linnhe and the Beauly Firth near Inverness, a distance of over 60 miles, taking in the lochs of Lochy, Oich and Ness. The road crosses the canal near the head of Neptune's Staircase, a series of eight locks which with three more locks at Corpach (see below) involves a fall of 80 feet to Loch Linnhe. B8004, ascending the west side of the Lochy and passing Torcastle, an old stronghold of the Mackin-toshes, leads to Gairlochy ($6\frac{1}{2}$ miles), with two more locks, at the foot of Loch Lochy, and thence towards Spean Bridge.

A830 on from Banavie to Corpach (1 mile).

Corpach, near the head of Loch Linnhe, has large new pulp and paper mills, and commands a wonderful view over the loch to the precipitous Ben Nevis. The road along Loch Eil and thence to Mallaig (the 'Road to the Isles') was first built by Thomas Tel-ford in the early 19th century.

A830 on by Loch Eil, passing Fassifern (see below), to Kin-locheil (8 miles).

Kinlocheil is near the west end of Loch Eil, a fine loch, 7 miles long and only $\frac{1}{2}$-$\frac{3}{4}$ mile broad, connected by a strait with Loch Linnhe. At Fassifern, among the trees at the foot of Glen Suileag, Prince Charles Edward was the guest of John Cameron after raising his standard at Glenfinnan. The road round the south shore of the loch to Camusnagaul (see Tour 2, page 17) branches to the left at the foot of Glen Fionnlighe.

A830 on to Glenfinnan ($6\frac{1}{2}$ miles).

Glenfinnan (hotel), one of the most beautiful and historic places in the Highlands, stands at the foot of the glen of that name and the upper end of Loch Shiel, a fresh-water loch over 18 miles long, down which there is an enchanting view. The shores of the loch, which is nowhere more than $\frac{3}{4}$ mile wide, are steep and rocky, and it is overlooked by impressive mountains, including Beinn Odhar Bheag (2895 feet), above the west shore, and Meall nan Creag Leac (2784 feet), rising from the east bank. A steamer plies down the loch on weekdays in summer to Acharacle, at the foot (Tour 2). Close to the loch head is the Glenfinnan Monument (admission daily, April to mid-October, 10 to dusk), or the Princes Charles Monument, believed to mark the spot where Prince Charles Edward unfurled his standard on 19th August, 1745, at the start of his attempt to regain the throne for the Stewarts, a campaign that ended disastrously on the field of Culloden (16th April, 1746). The monument was erected in 1815 by Alexander Macdonald of Glenaladale (a glen opening west of Loch Shiel), a descendant of one of the prince's followers with whom he had spent the night before the gathering. The statue of a kilted Highlander on the top looks north up the glens from which the clansmen, estimated at between 1,100 and 1,500 (Camerons, Macdonalds, Macdonells and many others), descended to support the Jacobite cause. The Glenfinnan Gathering and Highland Games are now held here annually on the Saturday nearest 19th August.

A830 on, ascending a green glen between steep-sided hills, then dropping down in wide curves and skirting the north shore of Loch Eilt (see below), for Lochailort (9½ miles).

Lochailort (hotel), at the junction of the new road from Kinloch-moidart (see Tour 2), lies about a mile from the foot of Loch Eilt, an enchanting small loch in a verdant glen, with several islets, and at the head of Loch Ailort, a beautiful sea-loch which opens with Loch nan Uamh (see below) into the lovely Sound of Arisaig, dotted with many islands. Into Loch nan Uamh ('loch of the caves'), Princes Charles Edward sailed on 26th July, 1745, in the French frigate, 'La Doutelle', with only seven companions. He had left France on 22nd June, unknown to his father, the 'Old Chevalier', and had stopped briefly at Eriskay, in the Outer Hebrides. The prince landed on the north shore of the loch at Borrodale on 4th August, and he set sail from the same place, after many wanderings, on 19th September, 1746.

A830 on, with many twists and turns, across a peninsula, passing the little Loch Dhu, touching the north shore of Loch nan Uamh, and crossing the Borrodale Burn near a memorial cairn set up in 1956, then going on to Arisaig (10½ miles).

Arisaig (hotel) is a small village on Loch nan Ceall or Cilltean, an inlet of the sea, with a splendid view of the mountainous island of Eigg to the west. Highland Games take place here in July.

A830 on across a wide moor, a popular camping place, over-looking white sandy beaches much frequented in summer for bathing, to Morar (6½ miles).

Morar (hotel) is a village on a small inlet famous for its beautiful white sands. Here are the workshops of the Highland Home Industries. The magnificent view out to sea includes the peaks of Rhum and the jagged Cuillins of Skye. The inlet is the mouth of the Morar River, flowing from Loch Morar, which, though only ½ mile from the road, is not visible from it. The loch, 11¼ miles long and ½-1½ miles wide, is no more than 30 feet above the sea, yet has a depth of over 1,000 feet and is, according to Sir Alexander Geikie, 'the deepest known hollow on any part of the European plateau except the submarine valley which skirts the south part of Scandinavia'. Simon Fraser, Lord Lovat, the last man to be beheaded in England (1747), was captured two months after Culloden on one of the group of islets near the west end.

A830 on, the last section on the mainland of the Road to the Isles ('By Ailort and by Morar to the sea'), to Mallaig (3 miles).

Mallaig (hotels) is an unprepossessing port and fishing village at the south end of the Sound of Sleat, and the terminus of the West

Highland Railway. From the enclosing cliffs there is an enticing view of Eigg, Rhum and the mountains of Skye, and another wonderful panorama is obtained from the rocky hill of Carn a' Ghobhair (1794 feet), to the east, where it takes in also Loch Morar and Loch Nevis, to the north, whose beautiful shores can be reached only on foot. Car Ferry services are operated to Armadale (see below), going on thence to Lochboisdale (on South Uist; Tour 5); steamers ply to Eigg and Rhum and to Kyle of Lochalsh and thence to Portree (on Skye) or to Stornoway (Tour 5); and day cruises are arranged in summer to Loch Hourn (north of Loch Nevis), Loch Duich, Loch Scavaig (below the Cuillins) and many other places. Highland Games are held at Mallaig in August.

The Car Ferry from the harbour crosses the Sound of Sleat to Armadale, with beautiful views into the steep-sided entrance to Loch Nevis, of the mountains to the north and of the Cuillins ahead.

Armadale lies on a small bay opening from the Sound of Sleat, which separates the southern arm of Skye from the mainland. The Gothic Armadale Castle, built about 1815, replaces the 'small house on the shore' where Johnson and Boswell were entertained by the Lord of the Macdonalds in 1773. A853 runs south to Ardvasar ($\frac{1}{2}$ mile; hotel), and a by-road goes on thence for $3\frac{1}{2}$ miles more to Aird of Sleat, from which a path continues for 2 miles to Point of Sleat, the south end of the fertile peninsula of Sleat and of Skye.

A851 north along the sound to Teangue ($4\frac{1}{2}$ miles).

Teangue lies on a bay of the Sound of Sleat near the ruined ivy-covered Knock Castle. From the road there are magnificent views across the sound to Loch Nevis (the 'loch of heaven') and the equally impressive Loch Hourn (the 'loch of hell'), farther north, with the peaks of Knoydart between them. A narrow by-road, leaving A851 1 mile north of Teangue, crosses the peninsula of Sleat to Ord ($4\frac{1}{2}$ miles farther; hotel), on Loch Eishort, for another magnificent view of the dramatic Cuillin Hills.

A851 on from Teangue to the small Loch nan Dubhrachan, where the road to Ord goes off, returning thence to the coast at Isleornsay ($3\frac{1}{2}$ miles).

Isleornsay (hotels) is a small bathing and fishing place taking its name from an offshore island. It faces across the sound into the superb entrance to Loch Hourn.

A851 on, skirting Loch na Dal, then across an open, desolate moorland and joining A850 in $7\frac{1}{2}$ miles; then left for 2 miles to Broadford, the starting point of Tour 4 (page 27).

Broadford (hotels) is a large but scattered village and a popular tourist centre on the wide Broadford Bay, on the north-east coast of Skye, looking across the Inner Sound to the Applecross mountains on the mainland. To the west rises Beinn na Caillich

(2400 feet), one of the Red Hills, singular masses of red granite. From Broadford, A881 runs south-west, past the loch (with its water-lilies) and the ruined church of Kilchrist, to Torrin (5½ miles), a small village on the fine inlet of Loch Slapin and at the south foot of the prominent Red Hills. Beyond the loch rise the impressive serrated peaks of Bla Bheinn, or Blaven (3042 feet), and Garbh Bheinn, or Garsven (2649 feet). A881, passing a limestone quarry, goes round the head of the loch and on (very hilly) to Elgol (9 miles more), a scattered village with a post office. A wonderful view opens from the cliffs and (better still) from the rocky shore at the foot, over Loch Scavaig to the jagged black ridges of the Cuillin Hills. Motor-boats may be hired from the jetty below Elgol to cross Loch Scavaig, above the head of which the dark Loch Coruisk, hemmed in by the formidable precipices of the Cuillins, may easily be reached on foot.

A850 back (east) from Broadford, near the coast of the Inner Sound, to Kyleakin (8½ miles).

Kyleakin (hotels) is a village of white houses on the Skye shore of the narrow strait of Kyle Akin, named after Hakon, King of Norway, who sailed through it in 1263 on his way to his defeat at the Battle of Largs (Ayrshire). The village stands on a promontory sheltering an inlet, overlooking the entrance to which are the tottering ruins of Castle Moil, a small tower-house traditionally built by the wife of a Macdonald and daughter of a Norwegian king who stretched a chain across the strait and attempted to levy a toll from passing ships.

Car Ferry across Kyle Akin, here only ½ mile wide, to Kyle of Lochalsh.

Kyle of Lochalsh (hotel) is a small port on the mainland, at the west or seaward end of Loch Alsh, up which there is a splendid view, and the terminus of the railway from Inverness. Steamers ply to Mallaig, Eigg and Rhum; to Toscaig, for the district of Applecross; to Portree, on Skye; and to Stornoway (Tour 5).

A87, turning inland and passing roads to Plockton (see below), to Balmacara (6 miles).

Balmacara (hotel) is the centre of a beautiful estate of 8,000 acres, bequeathed to the National Trust for Scotland in 1946 and covering most of the peninsula on which Kyle of Lochalsh stands. Balmacara House is now a school for boys who are specialising in crofting agriculture; and near the shore of Loch Alsh is an information centre. By-roads (see above) lead via Duirinish (hotel) to Plockton (hotels), a large fishing village situated on a bay of the beautiful Loch Carron. Another by-road leads from Duirinish to Strome Ferry (see below), passing through woods near the modern Duncraig Castle, now a school.

A87 on, near Loch Alsh to Auchtertyre (1½ miles), where the road to Strome Ferry goes off (see Tour 6). A87 on to Dornie

(3 miles) and thence via Loch Duich, Shiel Bridge, Glen Shiel and the Cluanie Inn to the upper end of Glen Moriston (31 miles more).

Dornie and the route thence to Glen Moriston are described in Tour 6 (pages 39-40).

A87 (right) crossing the River Moriston and ascending above the south side of Loch Loyne (see below) by a newly-constructed road, then across a range of moorland hills to descend to Loch Garry and through Glen Garry to Invergarry ($12\frac{1}{2}$ miles).

Invergarry (hotels) is a village enchantingly placed at the foot of Glen Garry in the Great Glen, and above the shores of Loch Oich, on a rock near which are the ruins of the Castle, a stronghold of the Macdonells of Glengarry. Loch Garry, in the charmingly wooded glen, and Loch Loyne have both been greatly extended by their inclusion in a large hydro-electric scheme. From Invergarry to Fort William the route runs through Glen More, or the Great Glen, the immense trench-like ravine which runs right across Scotland from Inverness.

A82 (right), skirting Loch Oich and crossing the Caledonian Canal at Laggan Locks (3 miles), then along the south-east shore of Loch Lochy to Invergloy (7 miles).

Loch Lochy is a narrow loch nearly 10 miles long, with steep shores mostly covered by woods. Farther on the road passes the Commando Memorial (1951), effectively placed, looking out over the rugged country where the commandos trained during the Second World War. From the memorial there is a splendid view of the stark precipices on the north face of the great mass of Ben Nevis, with deep gullies where snow lingers all the year round.

A82 on, turning away from the loch, to Spean Bridge (5 miles).

Spean Bridge (hotel) is a village on a fine reach of the Spean, at the foot of its long glen.

A82, turning right in the village, to Inverlochy (8 miles; see page 19), and thence to Fort William ($1\frac{1}{2}$ miles).

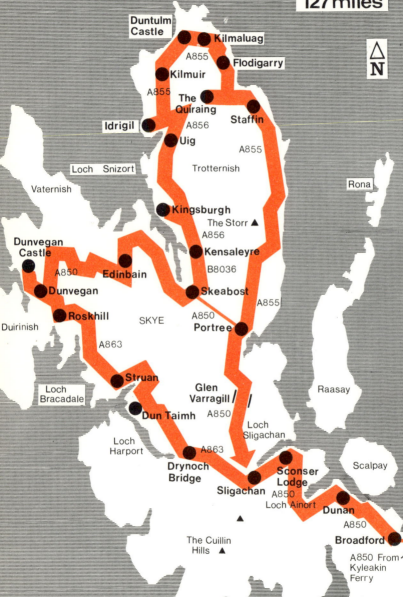

Tour 4
127 miles

△ N

Duntulm Castle · Kilmaluag · Flodigarry · A855 · Kilmuir · A855 · The Quiraing · Staffin · Idrigil · A856 · Uig · A855 · Loch Snizort · Trotternish · Vaternish · Rona · Kingsburgh · The Storr ▲ · A856 · Dunvegan Castle · Kensaleyre · A850 · Edinbain · B8036 · Dunvegan · Skeabost · Roskhill · SKYE · A850 · A855 · Duirinish · Portree · A863 · Struan · Raasay · Loch Bracadale · Dun Taimh · Glen Varragill · A850 · Loch Harport · Loch Sligachan · Drynoch Bridge · A863 · Sconser Lodge · Scalpay · Sligachan · A850 · Dunan · Loch Ainort · A850 · Broadford · The Cuillin Hills ▲ · A850 From Kyleakin Ferry

4. Round the Island of Skye

This tour covers much of Skye (the largest of the Hebrides after Lewis), a wild and beautiful island, though no longer as lonely and primitive as formerly. Its name is perhaps a corruption of 'sgaith', a wing, and so called from its shape. Skye is 50 miles in length from north to south, but its long and rugged coast is indented by many enchanting sea-lochs, breaking it up into a number of peninsulas, so that no part of the island is more than about 5 miles from the sea. In the south is the group of steep, black mountains known as the Cuillin Hills, or Coolins, whose jagged summits are the most fascinating rock scenery in Britain. The climate of Skye is mild and frequently damp, but this often results in beautiful and romantic mist effects. The island came under the domination of the Norsemen until the 13th century, and after this it was involved in the struggles between the 'Lords of the Isles' and the Crown, and in the interminable disputes between the Macdonalds, the Mackinnons and the MacLeods who laid claim to its territory. Prince Charles Edward Stewart sought refuge in Skye in 1746 after the disaster of Culloden, and in 1773 Dr. Johnson and James Boswell paid their famous visit to the island. Portree is the only town and the population is otherwise scattered among the many hamlets and farmsteads, though the croft system of farming, now on the decline, is supplemented by other employment. Skye is accessible from the mainland by way of the Car Ferries from Mallaig to Armadale and Kyle of Lochalsh to Kyleakin (see Tour 3). The roads on the island have been much improved in recent years.

Broadford, where this tour starts, is described in Tour 3 (page 23).
    A850 west, between the slopes of Beinn na Caillich (2400 feet) and the Caolas Scalpay, to Dunan (5 miles).

Dunan faces across the Caolas Scalpay, the strait, less than a mile wide, separating Skye from the island of Scalpay, which rises to 1298 feet in the Mullach nan Carn.
    A850 on round the south shore of the sheltered Loch Ainort, with a splendid view of the peaks to the south rising to Bla Bheinn, or Blaven (3042 feet). A new road cuts off the headland to the north of the loch and descends east of Glamaig to Sconser Lodge (8½ miles; hotel), on Loch Sligachan; the old road (2½ miles longer) rounds the north shore of Loch Ainort and the headland beyond to join the new road, which goes on to Sligachan (3 miles more).

Sligachan (hotel), at the junction of the roads to Portree (page 30) and Dunvegan, is a favoured angling and mountaineering centre, beautifully situated at the head of Loch Sligachan and the foot of the impressive Glen Sligachan, up which a track ascends south for the Cuillin Hills and Loch Coruisk. To the east rises Glamaig (2537 feet), a great cone of green syenite, and to the south-west is the pinnacle of Sgùrr nan Gillean (3167 feet), the northernmost of the Cuillins. Off the mouth of Loch Sligachan is the island of Raasay, 13½ miles long and rising to 1456 feet.

A863 on (west) from Sligachan over a moor, with enticing views of the Cuillins, then down Glen Drynoch to Drynoch Bridge (5½ miles).

Drynoch Bridge is at the head of the deep and narrow Loch Harport, a long inlet of the west coast of Skye. B8009 continues along the south shore of the loch to Merkadale (1½ miles) and Carbost (1 mile), which has a famous distillery, and thence to Port na Long (3 miles more), near the mouth of the loch, with a noted weaving industry. From Merkadale a rough and narrow road climbs over to Glen Brittle, which it descends to Glenbrittle House (7½ miles), a famous resort of climbers, who exercise their skills on Sgùrr Alasdair (3309 feet), the highest of the Cuillins, and other rocky peaks of this group, to the east.

A863 on from Drynoch Bridge, ascending above Loch Harport and passing Dun Taimh (5 miles), a good example of a fortified mound, before rounding the head of Loch Bracadale to Struan (3½ miles).

Struan (small hotels), with the Bracadale post office, is a scattered village above an arm of Loch Harport which opens to the broad Loch Bracadale, studded with many islands. Off Idrigill Point, which encloses the loch on the west, are three tall rocks or stacks of basalt known as Macleod's Maidens, and to the north-west are the curious flat-topped hills, called Macleod's Tables (1601 feet).

A863 on through a crofting district, rounding arms of Loch Bracadale to Roskhill (7 miles), then across the neck of the peninsula of Duirinish to Dunvegan (3 miles).

Dunvegan (hotels) is a village of white houses at the head of the seal-haunted Loch Dunvegan, a favourite sea-angling centre. Dunvegan Castle (admission weekdays, April to mid-October, 2 to 5), 1 mile north (by A850), is and has been for 700 years the seat of the MacLeod of MacLeod. Once accessible only from the loch, and now reached by a bridge across the former moat, the massive castle shows work of every period from the 14th century to the 19th. In the 14th-century Keep, which has walls 9 feet thick, is the dungeon, reached from the second floor near the drawing room. This has many interesting relics, including the Fairy Flag (of unknown origin), a silver-mounted Irish cup of bog-oak, and the Dunvegan Cup, the drinking horn of Rory Mòr MacLeod, the 16th chief, who was knighted by James VI. The South or Fairy Tower was built about 1500, the Central Tower, with the dining room, in 1623; the south wing was rebuilt in 1684-90 and the north wing, which has relics of Prince Charles Edward and Flora Macdonald, in 1791. The castle, which also contains portraits of chiefs by Allan Ramsay, Raeburn and

Zoffany, stands in an old-world garden of shrubs, in pleasant contrast to the open country around. From A863 south of Dunvegan, B884 leads west across the peninsula of Duirinish, and a rough by-road, branching right from this in 5½ miles, runs out towards the basalt cliffs of Dunvegan Head. Near Boreraig, 2 miles along this road, the MacCrimmons of Duirinish, hereditary pipers to the MacLeods, established a piping school in a hollow of the cliffs.

A850 east from Dunvegan, leaving a road on the left (B886) to Loch Bay and crossing the peninsula of Vaternish, with fine views from the open moorland, to Edinbain (8½ miles).

Edinbain (hotel) is a village at the head of Loch Greshornish, a narrow inlet of the larger Loch Snizort, between the Vaternish and Trotternish peninsulas.

A850 on to the head of Loch Snizort Beag at Skeabost (8½ miles; hotel), from which B8036 branches left to join A856 in 1½ miles, ½ mile short of Kensaleyre.

Kensaleyre is on an inlet east of Loch Snizort Beag. At Kingsburgh, farther on (see below), Prince Charles found refuge in 1746 in a house (since rebuilt) where Johnson and Boswell were later entertained by the laird and his wife, Flora Macdonald, the doctor sleeping in the prince's bed.

A856 on, passing above Kingsburgh House (3 miles; not seen from the road) and crossing Glen Hinnisdale, then descending to Uig (4½ miles more).

Uig (hotels), the starting point of the Car Ferry services to Lochmaddy (North Uist; see Tour 5) and to Tarbert (Harris), is a pleasant village spread round the charming Uig Bay, an opening on the east of Loch Snizort, enclosed on the north by the precipitous Ru Idrigil. A by-road on the right ascends above Uig in a sweeping zigzag to reach the ridge of Trotternish (5½ miles) above the Quiraing (see below).

A856 on round the bay towards Idrigil (1 mile) then A855 (right, with a sharp turn at first) to Kilmuir (4 miles farther).

Kilmuir is a long village above the north-west coast of Trotternish, affording a wide prospect over The Minch, the strait separating Skye from the Outer Hebrides. The Skye Cottage Museum, with old domestic utensils, agricultural implements, etc., is in an old 'black house' or crofter's cottage, occupied until 1958. Few of these black houses, once a characteristic feature of Skye, are now lived in, though some of them are used as barns. Farther up on the right is the graveyard of Kilmuir, with a conspicuous monument to Flora Macdonald, who helped Prince Charles Edward to escape, and who died at Kingsburgh in 1790; her grave here is inscribed with a tribute by Dr Johnson. On the shore near Monkstadt House, some distance south-west, the prince landed on 29th June, 1746, accompanied by Flora

Macdonald and disguised as 'Betty Burke', her maid, after a voyage from Benbecula, in the Outer Hebrides.

A855 on to Duntulm Castle (4 miles).

Duntulm Castle, now in ruins, was formerly a stronghold of the Macdonalds, Lords of the Isles. To the north is Rubha Hunish, the northernmost point of Trotternish and of Skye; from the hamlet of Kilmaluag, to the east, there is a fine view across The Minch to the hills of Harris and Lewis.

A855 on to Kilmaluag (1 mile) and thence to Flodigarry (3 miles more).

Flodigarry, above the east shore of Trotternish, has an hotel incorporating the early home of Flora Macdonald, who married Allan Macdonald of Kingsburgh in 1750. A fair road on the right 2 miles farther on ascends steeply to the Quiraing, an amazing mass of splintered towers that has broken away from the escarpment above. In a deep gully on the right of the road is the Needle, an imposing pinnacle about 120 feet high, while to the left is the Table, an inaccessible rock-tower with a grass-covered top. The view looking out from the Quiraing to the sea, with the mountains of Wester Ross beyond, is fascinating. The road zigzags up to the top of the ridge (2½ miles), for Uig (see above).

A855 on round Staffin Bay to Staffin (4 miles from Flodigarry).

Staffin (hotel) is a scattered farming community to the south of the sandy bay. The road returns to the cliffs farther on, where Loch Mealt pours its waters into the sea in a sheer cascade.

A855 on, passing Loch Mealt and continuing along the cliffs, rising thence towards the Old Man of Storr (9½ miles).

The Old Man of Storr is a black pinnacle of rock, 169 feet high, detached from the east foot of The Storr (2358 feet), a precipitous mountain forming the southern end and highest point of the long backbone of Trotternish.

A855 on past Loch Leathan and Loch Fada, linked in 1952 to form a reservoir for a hydro-electric scheme, and descending to Portree (8 miles).

Portree (hotels) is an attractive small town (the 'capital' of Skye), a fishing port and a tourist centre, built partly on the shore of Portree Bay, with a delightful harbour, but mostly on a platform of rock above this. It received its name (meaning 'king's haven') after a visit by James V. In the Royal Hotel is the room where Prince Charles said farewell to Flora Macdonald on 30th June, 1746. Steamers ply from Portree to Raasay, opposite the bay, and to Kyle of Lochalsh and Mallaig.

A850 on (south) ascending the long Glen Varragill, from the head of which there is a magnificent view of the Cuillins in front, then down to Sligachan (9½ miles; page 27) and on to Broadford (16½ miles more).

5. To the Outer Hebrides

The Outer Hebrides are a chain of islands, some 120 miles long, separated from the mainland and from Skye by a strait of 15-30 miles in width called The Minch. They may be divided into two groups, of which the northern, Lewis, or the Lews, by far the largest island (nearly 62 miles long and up to 28 miles wide), belongs to the county of Ross and Cromarty, except that its southern portion, called Harris, is included in Inverness-shire. To this county, too, belong the islands in the southern group, the chief of which, taken from north to south, are North Uist, Benbecula, South Uist and Barra. The islands have a long sea-board, facing the wild Atlantic but with many fine stretches of sandy beach; the coasts, especially on the eastern side, are split up by numerous sea-lochs, and offshore are innumerable small islands and barren islets. Inland, the country is broken up by a multiplicity of small lochs; otherwise the surface consists mainly of level moorland, though in Harris there are mountains rising to over 2,500 feet. The soil of the Outer Hebrides is poor and the Gaelic-speaking inhabitants are mostly occupied in fishing, the harvesting of seaweed and the manufacture of tweed, for which the islands are famous. The thatched 'black houses' or primitive crofters' cottages (see page 29), built of turf, without windows or a chimney, have now mostly disappeared, though some are in use as byres or barns. The Hebrides, known to the Norsemen as Sudreyjar, or Southern Islands, remained under their domination from the 8th century until 1266, when Magnus, Earl of Orkney, relinquished his claim to them. The 'Lord of the Isles' was a title first adopted by John Macdonald of Islay, but the power of the lords was slowly sapped by the Scottish kings and the title was eventually annexed to the Crown in 1495 by James IV. The Outer Hebrides may be reached by the Car Ferries from Uig (on Skye) to Tarbert (Harris) and to Lochmaddy (North Uist) and from Mallaig to Lochboisdale (South Uist) and by the steamers (carrying cars) from Oban and Tobermory to Castlebay (Barra) and Lochboisdale and from Mallaig and Kyle of Lochalsh to Stornoway, on Lewis, the only town in the islands. None of these services operates on Sundays. Roads on the islands are mostly narrow and winding, though with fair surfaces; causeways now connect Benbecula with North and South Uist.

Mallaig is described in Tour 3 (page 22).

The car ferry for Lochboisdale (on Fridays, in $4\frac{1}{4}$ hours) crosses the Sound of Sleat, calling at Armadale, in Skye, then rounds the Point of Sleat, with Eigg away to the left, and passes between Rhum and the south-west coast of Skye. There are splendid views of the mountains on all these islands. The ferry skirts the north side of Rhum, now a nature reserve, and the much smaller island of Canna, then steers west across The Minch to South Uist, on which Beinn Mhòr is seen rising to the right.

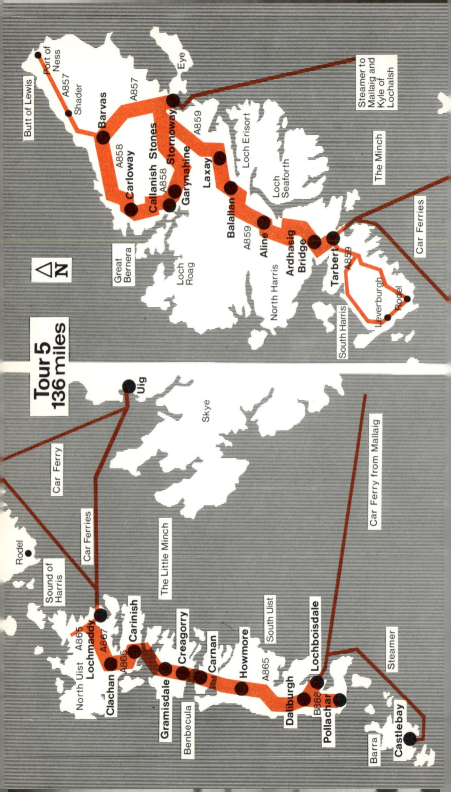

Lochboisdale (hotel), with a steamer pier on the loch of the same name, is a fishing village and the chief place on South Uist, an island 22 miles long and about 6-8 miles wide. A steamer (carrying cars) connects Lochboisdale three times a week (in 2 hours) with Barra, the southernmost of the larger islands, rounding the smaller Eriskay, noted for its folk-songs, where Prince Charles Edward first set foot on Scottish soil (23rd July, 1745). At the south end of Barra is Castlebay, a herring-fishing port with a harbour, and on a rocky islet in the bay here is the medieval Kisimul Castle (admission Saturdays, early May to early September, 3 to 6), reached from Castlebay by boat, the ancient seat of the Macneils of Barra, carefully restored by the present Macneil, the 45th chief. A road (A888; 12 miles) runs round the barren island, which is about 8 miles long, and a rough branch road leads from it to Traigh Mhòr, a sandy beach near the north end where aircraft landings are regularly made in connection with a service from Glasgow. To the south of Barra are the islands of Vatersay, Mingulay, with tall cliffs, and Berneray (with a lighthouse), the southernmost of the Outer Hebrides.

A865 west from Lochboisdale to Daliburgh (3 miles).

Daliburgh is at the junction of B888, which runs south to Pollachar (5 miles) for a view of Eriskay and Barra. At Milton, 4 miles north, near Loch Kildonan, are the remains of the birthplace (in 1722) of Flora Macdonald, whose first meeting with Prince Charles was at her brother's shieling at Alisary, on the other side of the road.

A865 north, along the length of South Uist, passing Loch Kildonan (on the left) and Beinn Mhòr (2034 feet), which rises to the right, to Howmore (10 miles; hotel) and thence across the shallow Loch Bee to Carnan ($7\frac{1}{2}$ miles).

Carnan is at the north end of South Uist. On the level country to the west of Loch Bee a large rocket range has been laid out since 1955; and on Rueval (286 feet), south of the loch, is a granite statue, 125 feet high, of Our Lady of the Isles, by Hew Lorimer (1954).

A865 on, over a causeway, replacing the South Ford, to Creagorry (1 mile).

Creagorry (hotel) is on the south shore of Benbecula, an island about 6 miles long by 8 miles wide, consisting mainly of a maze of small lochs. From the island Prince Charles sailed to Skye on 28th June, 1746, accompanied by Flora Macdonald.

A865 on to Gramisdale (6 miles), then across a causeway, replacing the North Ford, to Carinish (4 miles).

Carinish (small hotel) is on the south side of North Uist, an irregularly-shaped island 14 miles long by about 16 miles wide, nearly half of whose surface is covered by water.

A865 on to Clachan (3 miles) then A867 (right) among numerous lochs for 7½ miles more and A865 again (right) to Lochmaddy (1 mile).

Lochmaddy (hotels), the chief village on North Uist, stands on a loch of the same name which has innumerable islets and indentations. South Lee (920 feet), to the south, reached by boat, commands a view extending in clear weather from the Cuillins in Skye, over 40 miles south-east, to the rocky island of St. Kilda, over 50 miles north-west. Lochmaddy is connected by Car Ferry (five times weekly, in 2 hours) across The Minch and into Loch Snizort, for Uig, on Skye, which is also linked by Car Ferry (eleven times weekly, in 2 hours) with Tarbert.

From Lochmaddy by Car Ferry (twice weekly, in 2 hours) direct to Tarbert, on Harris, in connection with the service from Uig. The ferry emerges from Loch Maddy and crosses the east end of the Sound of Harris, a channel 5-8 miles wide, dotted with many small islands. Passing Renish Point, it skirts the coast of Harris and steams up East Loch Tarbert.

Tarbert (hotel), the principal village of Harris, stands on an isthmus hardly ½ mile wide separating the east and west lochs, and linking North and South Harris. Above West Loch Tarbert rises Ben Luskentyre (1654 feet). A859, a roundabout road, runs along the east coast of South Harris at first, then crosses to the west for Glen Laxdale, remarkable for its 'funeral cairns' used by coffin bearers, and Luskentyre Bay, with its silver sands. The road continues down the west coast to Scarastavore, where the distinctive peninsula of Toe Head is seen beyond another sandy bay, and thence to Leverburgh, or Obbe (21 miles), on the delightful Sound of Harris, where Lord Leverhulme attempted to establish a fishing station. A859 goes on to Rodel (3 miles), near Renish Point, with the restored Church of St. Clement, built about 1500 and containing fine tombs of the MacLeods, including Alastair MacLeod of Dunvegan, with an effigy in armour (1528), and Donald MacLeod of Berneray, who fought for Prince Charles Edward. A narrow, hilly road, with many sharp bends, runs along the east coast from Rodel towards Tarbert.

A859 west from Tarbert, skirting the west loch to Ardhasig Bridge (3½ miles).

Ardhasig Bridge is on an arm of West Loch Tarbert, to the north of which rises a range of rock-strewn mountains culminating in Clisham (2622 feet), the highest peak in the Outer Hebrides. B887 runs along the north shore of the loch to Amhuinnsuidhe Castle (9 miles), where Sir James Barrie wrote part of *Mary Rose,* and thence to Husinish Bay (4½ miles farther), opposite the mouth of the loch.

A859, climbing away from the loch to the high ridge between Clisham (of which there is a fine view) and Sgaoth Ard (1829 feet), then descending to the shore of Loch Seaforth at Ardvourlie Castle (8 miles).

Loch Seaforth is a long fjord-like inlet that gave its name to the Seaforth Highlanders, a regiment raised by a Mackenzie whose hunting-ground was in this neighbourhood.

A859 on, crossing the boundary between the districts of Harris and Lewis at Aline ($1\frac{1}{2}$ miles), and thence through a region of numerous small lochs to Balallan ($9\frac{1}{2}$ miles more).

Balallan is at the head of Loch Erisort, another delightful sea-loch. B8060 runs along the south shore, then turns away south for Lemreway, on an inlet at the mouth of the remote Loch Shell (13 miles).

A859 on, north of Loch Erisort, to Laxay (3 miles) and through a region of moorland and lochs for 10 miles; then A858 (right) and A857 (right again) to Stornoway (2 miles farther).

Stornoway (several hotels), the largest town in the Hebrides and in Ross and Cromarty, is an important herring-fishing port, with a fine harbour, and has famous manufactures of tweeds. The Episcopalian Church of St. Peter preserves a red-granite font of unknown age and the prayer book of David Livingstone, the missionary and explorer. To the west of the harbour, in wooded grounds noted for their rhododendrons, is the 19th-century Lewis or Lews Castle (now a technical college), formerly the home of Lord Leverhulme, who attempted to modernise the methods of farming and fishing on the island. Farther south, beyond the River Creed, is Arnish Lighthouse, at the harbour entrance, where a cairn commemorates a night spent in a farm by Prince Charles during his wanderings after Culloden. A866 runs east past the airport and across the isthmus connecting the town with the Eye Peninsula, where the ruined church of Eye, at the end of the causeway, contains monuments of the MacLeods.

A857 north from Stornoway, then A858 left again, over open moorland to Garynahine ($13\frac{1}{2}$ miles).

Garynahine is a small fishing port on the inner reach of East Loch Roag. B8011 leads south-west from here, round the head of the loch (beyond which B8059 branches right for the bridge to the island of Great Bernera) to the head of Little Loch Roag, then turns north, through little-visited country, to the western arm of Loch Roag and to Uig ($19\frac{1}{2}$ miles), on a large sandy inlet.

A858 on from Garynahine, passing east of the Callanish Stones (2 miles).

The Callanish Standing Stones, the most remarkable monument of their kind in Scotland, consist of a chambered burial cairn with a monolith nearly 16 feet high opposite the entrance, surrounded by a circle of stones, nearly 40 feet in diameter, from which other rows or avenues of stones fan out. There are 46 stones in all, and the monument, which was presumably intended to serve some ritual purpose, measures about 400 feet from end to end.

A858 on along the east side of East Loch Roag to Carloway (6½ miles).

Carloway (hotel) is a crofting village near the head of the small Loch Carloway, to the south of which is Dun Carloway, a well-preserved example of a broch (see page 60), 30 feet high.

A858 on near the north coast of Lewis, through a crofting district with many sandy bays, to Barvas (12 miles).

Barvas stands on A857, which runs north to Shader (4 miles), with the Clach an Trushal, a monolith 20 feet high. To the right, near the small Loch an Duin, is the Steinacleit cairn and stone circle, of the Neolithic Age. A857 goes on to Port of Ness (11 miles; hotel), which has a small harbour, where B8015 leads left towards the Butt of Lewis (2½ miles), with a lighthouse, the northernmost point of Lewis and of the Hebrides, its rocky cliffs inhabited by sea-birds.

A857 right (south) from Barvas, crossing a moorland region to Stornoway (12 miles), for the steamer to Kyle of Lochalsh or Mallaig, or the road back to Tarbert.

6. From the Great Glen to the Atlantic Coast

This tour, starting from Inverness, the 'capital of the Highlands' and a focal point of northern Scotland, traverses the Great Glen, or Glen More (page 25), at first, skirting the delightful Loch Ness as far as Invermoriston. The route then crosses by Glen Moriston and Glen Shiel, one of the few breaches in the almost impenetrable Highland barrier, to reach the Atlantic coast at Loch Duich, in a region of beautiful sea-lochs. It turns off the Kyle of Lochalsh road, one of the 'Roads to the Isles' (see Tour 3), and crosses Loch Carron at Strome Ferry. (This ferry operates only on weekdays and can carry a limited number of cars; though the services are frequent, a long wait can often be anticipated in summer—as much as 2 hours in the height of the season. This, however, will be avoided when the new road along the south shore of Loch Carron is complete). The return to Inverness is made by Glen Carron and Strath Bran, another Highland breach, towards Strathpeffer (on Tour 8) and then round the Beauly Firth.

Inverness (numerous hotels), a busy tourist and commercial centre and a royal burgh, mainly of modern aspect, is well situated on the River Ness, $4\frac{1}{2}$ miles below the foot of its loch and about 1 mile from the mouth of the river in the Moray Firth. The large Castle, rebuilt in 1834-46 as the county offices and law courts, replaces the old castle in which Shakespeare laid scenes in *Macbeth*. On the Castle Hill, which affords a charming view up the Ness, is a statue of Flora Macdonald, who assisted Prince Charles Edward in his escape after the battle of Culloden. The fine Museum and Art Gallery (admission weekdays, 10 to 12.45 and 2.15 to 5.15), built in 1966, has notable Highland collections and Jacobite relics. Old building in Inverness include Queen Mary's House, in Bridge Street, where the Queen of Scots lodged when she was refused admission to the castle, and the late-16th-century Abertarff House (now the northern headquarters of the Highland Association) and the 17th-century Dunbar's Hospital, both in Church Street. In the same churchyard are the High Parish Church and the Greyfriars Free Church (formerly the Old Gaelic Church), both of the late 18th century. On the west bank of the river is the dignified St. Andrew's Cathedral (admission daily, 9 to 9), built in 1869, for the episcopal see of Moray, Ross and Caithness. The Northern Meeting, held near by in September, is noted for its Highland Games and other characteristic Scottish events.

A82, leaving Inverness on the south-west by Tomnahurich Street and Glen Urquhart Road, through the valley of the Ness and along the shore of Loch Ness to Drumnadrochit (15 miles).

Loch Ness, 23 miles long and over 900 feet deep in places, is one of the longest inland lochs in Scotland and a major link in the

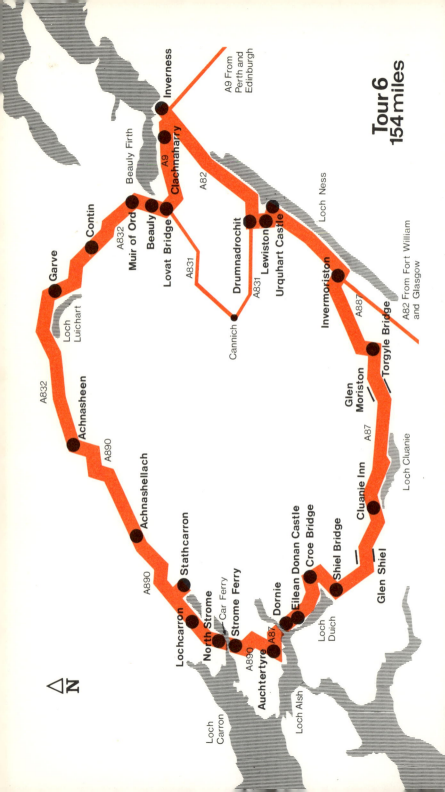

Tour 6
154 miles

N

A9 From Perth and Edinburgh

Inverness
Clachnaharry
Beauly Firth
A9
A82
Muir of Ord
Beauly
Contin
Lovat Bridge
Garve
A832
A831
Drumnadrochit
Lewiston
Urquhart Castle
Loch Ness
Loch Luichart
Cannich
A831
A82 From Fort William and Glasgow
A832
Achnasheen
Invermoriston
A887
A890
Torgyle Bridge
Glen Moriston
Achnashellach
A87
Loch Cluanie
Stathcarron
A890
Cluanie Inn
Lochcarron
Car Ferry
North Strome
Strome Ferry
Croe Bridge
Shiel Bridge
A87
Dornie
Eilean Donan Castle
Glen Shiel
Auchtertyre
A890
Loch Duich
Loch Carron
Loch Alsh

Caledonian Canal scheme (see page 20). Its shores, enclosed by moorland hills, are now mostly clothed with plantations. The loch, which has never been known to freeze, is famous for its 'monster', about which there are many stories but no conclusive evidence. Drumnadrochit (hotels) is a pleasant village in the lower part of Glen Urquhart, which opens to the loch in Urquhart Bay.

A82 on to Lewiston (1 mile), returning thence above the loch shore near Urquhart Castle (1 mile more).

Urquhart Castle (admission 10 to 7; October-March, 10 to 4: Sundays from 2), dramatically placed on a bold promontory above Loch Ness, south of Urquhart Bay, is a large and impressive ruin, mostly of the 16th-17th centuries, but incorporating a fortification of the 12th century and later, seized and strengthened in 1296 by Edward I, and given in 1509 by James IV to the Seafield Grants. Beside the shore road over 1 mile farther on is a memorial to John Cobb, who lost his life on the loch in 1952 while attempting to break the water speed record of 206 m.p.h.

A82 on beside Loch Ness, passing the Cobb Memorial, to Invermoriston (10½ miles).

Invermoriston (hotel) is a small village exquisitely situated near the foot of the wooded Glen Moriston. For the continuation of A82 via Fort Augustus to Invergarry (Tour 3), see Letts Motor Tour Guide to *The Highlands from Edinburgh to Inverness.*

A887 (right), running west up Glen Moriston to Torgyle Bridge (8½ miles).

Glen Moriston, whose river has been utilised in a hydro-electric scheme, is beautifully forested in its lower reaches, below Torgyle Bridge. Farther on, near the mouth of the River Doe, is a monument to Roderick Mackenzie, a young Edinburgh lawyer, who allowed the Hanoverian soldiers who captured him to think he was Prince Charlie, and in consequence was beheaded. In a cave up the glen of the Doe, the prince hid for five days in August, 1746.

A887 on to the head of Glen Moriston (6½ miles) where the road from Invergarry comes in, then A87 on through open moorland and above Loch Cluanie to Cluanie Bridge (9½ miles) and the new Cluanie Inn.

Loch Cluanie, a long and desolate sheet of water, has been much enlarged by its conversion into a reservoir as part of the large hydro-electric scheme. Cluanie Bridge is near the west end, with the solitary inn farther on.

A87 on down the wild and magnificent Glen Shiel, overlooked on each side by great mountain ranges, to Shiel Bridge (12 miles).

Shiel Bridge (hotels), or Invershiel, is a village delightfully situated at the foot of Glen Shiel and near the head of the fascinating Loch Duich, backed by the Five Sisters of Kintail, a range of sharp peaks whose highest point is Sgùrr Fhuaran (3505 feet), or Scour Ouran. The National Trust for Scotland owns 15,000 acres of the Kintail estate, including Beinn Fhada, or Ben Attow, to the east. A by-road runs along the south shore of the loch to Totaig (6 miles), which is connected by a passenger ferry across the upper reach of Loch Alsh to Ardelve (see below). Another road, diverging left from this in less than 1 mile, crosses the pass of Mam Ratagan (1116 feet), which is still, as Johnson and Boswell found it, 'a terrible steep to climb'. The road goes on to Glenelg ($8\frac{1}{2}$ miles from Shiel Bridge), a small village on a bay at the head of the Sound of Sleat where it narrows to the beautiful ravine of Kyle Rhea. A Car Ferry crosses (in summer; no reservations) to the hamlet of Kylerhea, on Skye, from which a steep and narrow road climbs through Glen Arroch to the road between Kyleakin and Broadford (Tour 3).

A87 on, to round an arm of Loch Duich at Croe Bridge ($2\frac{1}{2}$ miles), below the western ridge of Ben Attow (the 'long mountain'), then above the north side of the loch by a steep and hilly road, descending to the shore and passing Eilean Donan Castle before reaching Dornie (7 miles more).

Dornie (hotel) is a village at the junction of Loch Long with the magnificent Loch Duich, one of the grandest sea-lochs in Scotland, to form Loch Alsh. Eilean Donan Castle (admission weekdays, April to October, 10 to 12.30 and 2 to 6; tea-room), on a rocky islet connected with the shore by a bridge, was built in 1220 by Alexander II and became a stronghold of the Mackenzies, Earls of Seaforth. In 1719 it was garrisoned by Spanish Jacobite troops and battered by an English warship. The castle was well restored in 1932 by Colonel MacRae, a descendant of the last constable, and contains interesting Jacobite relics. From the road along the loch shore there is a splendid view of the Five Sisters of Kintail.

A87 on across the mouth of Loch Long to Ardelve (1 mile; hotel), on the north shore of Loch Alsh, and thence to Auchtertyre (2 miles more); then A890 (right), a hilly road with charming views, to Strome Ferry (7 miles farther; hotel), for the Car Ferry (weekdays only; no reservations) to North Strome, or Stromemore.

Strome Ferry crosses Loch Carron, a large and beautiful sea-loch, here narrowing to only $\frac{1}{2}$ mile. On the shore at North Strome are the remains of a castle. A new road now being built on the south shore will obviate the ferry crossing, but will miss the village of Lochcarron.

A890 on by the north shore to Lochcarron ($4\frac{1}{2}$ miles).

Lochcarron (hotels), formerly called Jeantown, is a fishing village pleasantly situated on the shore of the loch, and is the starting point of Tour 7.

A890 on by Loch Carron, then past the end of a road (B856) to Strathcarron station (hotel; on the new road), and on up the strath to Achnashellach (8 miles).

Achnashellach (hotels) is on the small Loch Dughaill or Doule where the strath narrows to Glen Carron. On the north-west are rugged mountains rising to Sgùrr Ruadh (3142 feet).

A890 on through Glen Carron, then down past Loch Gowan to Achnasheen (13 miles).

Achnasheen is in Strath Bran, at the junction of the road from Kinlochewe and Loch Maree (Tour 7), with the fine peak of Fionn Bheinn (3059 feet) rising to the north.

A832 right, descending the strath to Loch Achanalt, then rounding the north side of Loch Luichart to Garve (16½ miles), at the junction of the road from Ullapool (Tour 8), and thence to Contin (6½ miles).

Garve and the road thence to Contin (for Strathpeffer) are described in Tour 8 (page 49).

A832 on over the Conon to Marybank (2½ miles), then across a wooded strath to Muir of Ord (4½ miles more).

Muir of Ord (hotels), a village on the main road (A9) from Dingwall to Inverness, is the centre of a crofting district and was once noted for its large cattle fairs.

A9 (right) across the strath to Beauly (2½ miles).

Beauly (hotels), a pleasant small town on the River Beauly, takes its name from a priory ('de bello loco'), founded in 1230 by Sir John Bisset of the Aird for Valliscaulian monks from France. Of this there survives the ruined Priory Church (admission 10 to 7; October-March to 4; Sundays from 2), in a churchyard with some fine old trees at the north end of the wide main street. The west front, with its three lancets, was rebuilt after 1530 by Abbot Reid, Bishop of Orkney; in the south wall of the nave are three remarkable triangular windows of the 13th century. The chancel has unusual window arcading; the north transept, restored in 1901, is the burial-place of the Mackenzies of Kintail.

A9 on to Lovat Bridge (1 mile).

Lovat Bridge crosses the River Beauly at the foot of the beautifully wooded glen up which A831 runs to Kilmorack church (1½ miles). A by-road, crossing the river near here, passes the entrance to Beaufort Castle, the 19th-century baronial mansion of Lord Lovat, the chief of the Frasers, standing among extensive woods. The charming road goes on up the south side of glen to join the Drumnadrochit road near Cannich. A831 continues on the north side of the glen of the Beauly, whose waters have been utilised in a large hydro-electric scheme, the dam for which is at the lower end of the fine gorge of The Dhruim, with its richly wooded crags and curious rocks rising direct from the river. The once-famous falls of the Beauly have been swallowed up by the raising of the water-level. Near the Crask of Aigas (2½ miles from Kilmorack) is Eilean Aigas, an island which separates two branches of the river. The small house on it became a refuge of Lord Lovat in 1697 and was the summer home of Sir Robert Peel, the Prime Minister, before his death in 1850. Erchless Castle, a Scottish baronial mansion 4½ miles farther up, was once the seat of The Chisholm, the chief of the clan that from the 14th century owned the country round Strathglass, into which the road emerges beyond the hamlet of Struy, ½ mile farther on. Cannich (hotels), at the upper end of A831 and 16 miles from Lovat Bridge, is a village on the Glass, as the upper reach of the River Beauly is named, in the broad flat-bottomed strath, surrounded by beautiful woods. An unclassified road to the north-west climbs through Glen Cannich ('glen of the cotton-grass'), amid grand scenery, to the dam (9 miles) at the foot of Loch Mullardoch, an enlarged loch (now 9 miles long) that is incorporated in a vast hydro-electric scheme inaugurated in 1952. The power-station for this is at Fasnakyle, 2½ miles south-west of Cannich on the new road that ascends the delightful Glen Affric, which has been proposed as the nucleus of a National Park, the first in Scotland. The road goes on through the wooded Chisholm's Pass to reach the dam at the foot of Loch Benevean or Beinn a' Mheadhoin, then skirts the north shore to its present end (11 miles from Cannich) between this loch and Loch Affric, among some of the most impressive scenery in the Highlands. From Cannich, A831 turns east, passing the small Loch Meiklie and descending Glen Urquhart, through charming woods, to Drumnadrochit (16 miles; page 39).

A9 east from Lovat Bridge, crossing the River Beauly, then farther on skirting the southern shore of the Beauly Firth to Clachnaharry (9½ miles).

Clachnaharry is at the northern end of the Caledonian Canal (page 21), which descends six locks to enter the sea in the Beauly Firth. The shore road affords fine views over the firth to the Black Isle.

A9 on to enter Inverness (2 miles) by Telford Street and Kenneth Street, from which Tomnahurich Street leads left towards the Ness Bridge.

7. The Western Seaboard from Loch Carron to Little Loch Broom

This tour, starting from the village of Lochcarron, explores the coast of Wester Ross nearly as far north as Ullapool, on Loch Broom, a region of enchanting sea-lochs backed by the formidable Highland barrier, which is breached in this section only by the line of Glen Carron and Strath Bran and the glen extending Loch Broom south-eastward. The tour may be started from Dornie (Tour 6) or from Kyle of Lochalsh (Tour 3), but in both cases this involves crossing the Strome Ferry until the new road on the south shore of Loch Carron is complete (see page 40).

Lochcarron village is described in Tour 6 (page 40).

A896 north and west, crossing the steep ridge, with extensive views, to Kishorn ($4\frac{1}{2}$ miles).

Kishorn is on Loch Kishorn, an inlet of the larger Loch Carron, with a magnificent view south-west over the mouth of this loch and the Inner Sound to the mountains of Skye, while to the north-west rises the double mountain of Sgùrr a' Chaorachain (2539 feet) and Beinn Bhàn (2936 feet), in the peninsula of Applecross, where the red Torridonian sandstone is well seen. An unclassified road, leaving the main road at Tornapress (see below), rounds the head of Loch Kishorn, then climbs steeply by zigzags (no passing places) to the head of the Bealach nam Bo (2054 feet), or Pass of the Cattle, west of Sgùrr a' Chaorachain. One of the highest road passes in Scotland, this commands splendid views south over Loch Carron to the mountains around Loch Alsh and Loch Duich, and westward to Skye and the Outer Hebrides. The descent is made by easier gradients to reach the sea at Applecross ($13\frac{1}{2}$ miles from Kishorn; small hotel), a village on the west of the peninsula, facing across the Inner Sound to the long island of Raasay and to Skye. The name is in Gaelic 'A' Chomraich', i.e. 'The Sanctuary', from a monastery founded in 673 by Maelrubha, or Maree, a monk from Bangor, in Ireland. Of this there remains a slab carved with a cross near a ruined church on the north shore of the bay. The road goes on south near the coast to Toscaig (4 miles), which is connected by steamer with Kyle of Lochalsh.

A896 on from Kishorn to Tornapress (2 miles), then up a wild glen east of the great corries on Beinn Bhàn, and down through Glen Shieldaig, partly afforested, to Shieldaig ($8\frac{1}{2}$ miles more).

Shieldaig is a fishing village beautifully positioned on Loch Shieldaig, a deep inlet opening to the middle section of Loch Torridon. To the north-east rise the imposing Torridonian peaks of Beinn Alligin and Liathach.

A896 (a fine new road) above the south shore of the beautiful Upper Loch Torridon to Torridon (8 miles).

Torridon (hotel) is a scattered community rather than a village,

Tour 7
155 miles

N

A832 From Inverness
Garve
A835
Loch Glascarnoch
A835
Loch Luichart
Braemore Lodge
Achnasheen
A832
A890
A832
Dundonnell
Little Loch Broom
Achnashellach
Inverewe Gardens
Loch Maree
A896
Kinlochewe
Strathcarron
Gruinard Bay
Aultbea
Laide
Torridon
A890 From Fort William
Loch Ewe
Poolewe
A832
A890
Lochcarron
Gairloch
Kerrysdale
Shieldaig
Kishorn
A896
Loch Gairloch
Applecross
Loch Carron
Loch Torridon

round the head of the loch and at the foot of a wide, level strath, in one of the most enchanting situations in the Highlands. It is hemmed in by towering heights culminating on the north in the wild Liathach (3456 feet), a mountain with massive crags of red Torridonian sandstone, capped with white quartzite (best seen in the setting sun). A narrow road runs along the north shore of Upper Loch Torridon to Inveralligin (5 miles), beneath Beinn Alligin (3232 feet), and thence (rough and hilly) to Diabaig (4½ miles farther), on the lower section of Loch Torridon. The main road, ascending the rugged Glen Torridon (see below), is overshadowed by the giant precipices of Beinn Eighe.

A896 up Glen Torridon to the charming Loch Clair and thence to Kinlochewe (11 miles).

Kinlochewe (hotels) is a hamlet on a strath near the foot of Glen Docherty and 2 miles from the head of Loch Maree. To the west rises the impressive Beinn Eighe (3309 feet), or Ben Eay, the 'file mountain', a mass of Torridonian sandstone topped by a cone of white quartzite by which it is 'powdered with its own dust'. Over 10,000 acres of its east slopes, between Loch Clair and Loch Maree, the home of the wild cat, the pine marten and the golden eagle, are now the Beinn Eighe Nature Reserve, created in 1951 and the first of its kind in Britain. The road (A832) up Glen Docherty goes on to Achnasheen (9½ miles; see page 47).

A832 (narrow, with passing places) north-west from Kinlochewe, skirting the south shore of Loch Maree to its hotel (10 miles).

Loch Maree, over 12 miles long, is one of the largest and loveliest inland lochs in Scotland. It was probably once an extension of Loch Ewe (from which, presumably, Kinlochewe is named). Overlooking the upper end are the great crags on Beinn a' Mhùinidh (2231 feet) and the long rifts and gullies on the immense cone of Slioch (3217 feet), while the Beinn Eighe group rises impressively to the south. Towards its north end the loch widens out to over 2 miles, and here are several wooded islands, one of which is said to have been the retreat of St. Maelrubha or Maree.

A832 on, turning west, away from Loch Maree, among rich woods, and through the narrow pass of Kerrysdale (7 miles).

Kerrysdale opens to the inner end of the broad Loch Gairloch. B8056, on the left here, rounds the south side of the loch to Port Henderson (4½ miles), then runs down the coast to Redpoint (3½ miles), near the mouth of Loch Torridon. This road affords fine views over The Minch to the long ridge of the peninsula of Trotternish, in Skye, and to the island of Lewis, farther off.

A832 on from Kerrysdale, east of Loch Gairloch, to Gairloch (3 miles).

Gairloch (hotels) is a scattered village on the shore of its sea-loch, with sandy beaches and a superb retrospect of the mountains around Loch Maree and Loch Torridon. B8021, leading west round the loch and then along the coast to Melvaig (10 miles), affords another wide view over The Minch.

A832 on from Gairloch, recrossing the isthmus between Loch Maree and the sea, with a view that includes the islands of Skye and Lewis, to Poolewe (6 miles).

Poolewe (hotels), at the mouth of the Ewe, which drains Loch Maree into Loch Ewe, is named from a pool through which the river reaches the sea. The splendid view up the great trough that contains Loch Maree includes the steep-faced Beinn Airigh Charr (2593 feet) and Beinn Lair (2817 feet), with Slioch and Beinn Eighe farther away. On the east side of the bay of Poolewe is Inverewe House, famous for its sub-tropical gardens (admission weekdays, 10 to dusk; Sundays, 1 to dusk; tea-room), first laid out by Osgood Mackenzie from 1862 on, and now the property of the National Trust for Scotland. These beautiful and secluded gardens (best seen in late May and early June), enjoy the mild and soft air of the western seaboard of Scotland, and they contain many trees and shrubs rare in Britain. B8057 runs north from Poolewe, along the west shore of Loch Ewe to its mouth (9 miles).

A832 from Poolewe, passing the entrance to the Inverewe Gardens (1 mile; see above) and running east of Loch Ewe to Aultbea (4½ miles more; hotels), which has a naval station beside the loch; then across another isthmus commanding grand sea views to Laide (3½ miles), on the west side of Gruinard Bay.

Gruinard Bay is a broad inlet of the sea, with a beautiful sandy beach; the entrance to Little Loch Broom opens on the east side. From Laide, on the west side, there is a fine view of the Beinn Lair group, to the south, of Beinn Dearg Mhòr and the cone of An Teallach, to the east, and of the Coigach Hills beyond the bay.

A832 on round the bay, crossing the Gruinard River, then up a defile and along the slopes above the south shore of Little Loch Broom by a new road for Dundonnell (16 miles).

Dundonnell (hotel) lies above the head of Little Loch Broom, which is 9 miles long, and below the steep slopes of An Teallach (3484 feet), meaning 'The Forge', a magnificent mountain of the red Torridonian sandstone.

A832, up the deep and narrow ravine of the Dundonnell River, with a splendid retrospect of the wild An Teallach, to reach a height of 1110 feet, then on down to Braemore Lodge (13½ miles); then A835 right (east) to Garve (19½ miles).

Braemore Lodge and the road thence to Garve are described in Tour 8 (page 49).

A832 right (west) through Strath Bran to Achnasheen (16¼ miles), then A890 left to Lochcarron village (21 miles farther).

Achnasheen and the road from Garve to Lochcarron are described in Tour 6 (pages 40-41).

8. From Inverness across the Black Isle to Loch Broom

This tour crosses the county of Ross and Cromarty from the east coast to the west, from the Beauly Firth and the Black Isle to the coast at Ullapool, on Loch Broom, from which the return route breaches the great Highland barrier by Strath Oykel. An alternative start from Inverness, avoiding the Kessock Ferry (which operates daily across the Beauly Firth), follows A9 (very busy in summer) via Beauly and Muir of Ord, from which A832 runs north-west to Contin (Tour 6), but this misses both Dingwall and Strathpeffer. The roads are mostly hilly and narrow (though with passing places) between Garve and Ullapool and thence to Ledmore and Bonar Bridge, but many improvements to the width and surface have recently been made. The return route from Bonar Bridge via Dingwall runs mainly through an agricultural landscape, with views across the Dornoch and Cromarty Firths.

Inverness is described in Tour 6 (page 37).

B9161 north from Church Street, crossing the Ness by Waterloo Bridge, then via Kessock Street and Road to South Kessock (2 miles), for the Car Ferry across the Beauly Firth to North Kessock.

North Kessock is a village on the shore of the firth just above the place where it narrows before opening out again as the inner reach of the Moray Firth. From here a long detour (31 miles) may be made round the Black Isle, the broad, fertile promontory between these firths and the Cromarty Firth. It follows B9161 (see below) to Munlochy (5 miles) and A832 thence (right) to Fortrose (5½ miles more; hotels), a quiet resort and old royal burgh on the inner reach of the Moray Firth, with a ruined red sandstone Cathedral (admission on application to the custodian), part of the church founded in the 13th century for the see of Ross. A832 goes on to Rosemarkie (1 mile; hotels), a small but attractive resort with a sandy bathing beach on the outer reach of the Moray Firth, facing across the narrows to Fort George, and thence to Cromarty (9 miles more; hotel), once a royal burgh, with old houses and a small harbour on the Cromarty Firth near its narrow entrance from the Moray Firth. Hugh Miller's Cottage (admission weekdays, March to November, 10 to 12 and 2 to 5), a thatched cottage of 1650 in Church Street, was the birthplace in 1802 of the stonemason and geologist who made the Black Isle famous; it is now a museum. B9163, along the south shore of the Cromarty Firth and north of Millbuie, a long wood-covered ridge, leads to Conon Bridge (20 miles; see below).

B9161 from North Kessock for 2 miles, then B9162 on to Tore (2½ miles more), on A832 (connecting Muir of Ord with Fortrose), and B9162 on again, over the Black Isle to Conon Bridge (5 miles farther).

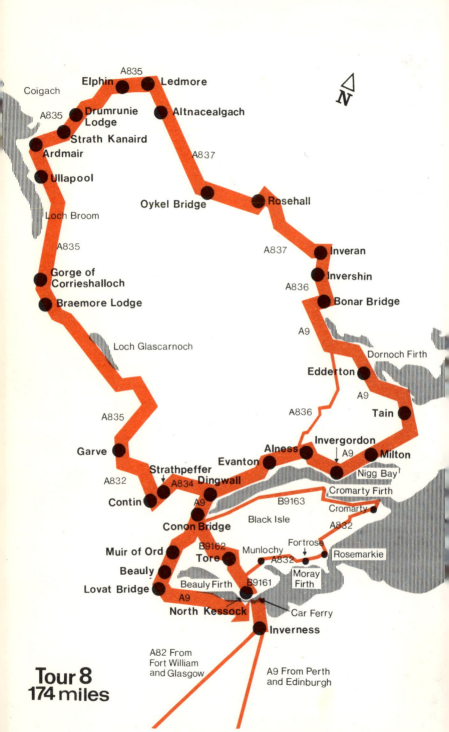

Coigach

Elphin A835 **Ledmore**

A835 **Drumrunie Lodge**

Strath Kanaird

Altnacealgach

Ardmair

A837

Ullapool

Oykel Bridge **Rosehall**

Loch Broom

A837 **Inveran**

A835 **Invershin**

A836

Bonar Bridge

Gorge of Corrieshalloch

A9

Braemore Lodge

Dornoch Firth

Loch Glascarnoch

Edderton

A9

A836

Tain

A835

Garve

Invergordon

A832

Strathpeffer

Alness

Evanton

A9

Milton

Dingwall

Nigg Bay

A834

Contin

Cromarty Firth

A9

B9163

Cromarty

Conon Bridge

Black Isle

A832

B9162

Muir of Ord

Fortrose

Tore

Munlochy

Rosemarkie

Beauly

A832

Lovat Bridge

Moray Firth

Beauly Firth

B9161

A9

North Kessock

Car Ferry

Inverness

A82 From Fort William and Glasgow

A9 From Perth and Edinburgh

Tour 8 174 miles

N

Conon Bridge (hotel) is a small angling resort at the lower end of Strath Conon and on the south side of the River Conon at its entrance into the Cromarty Firth. It has a splendid view of the massive Ben Wyvis to the north.

A9 on to Dingwall (2½ miles).

Dingwall (hotels), near the head of the firth, is a market centre and the busy county town of Ross and Cromarty. Its old buildings include the Town House in the High Street, partly of 1730. Dingwall, created a royal burgh in 1226 by Alexander II, takes its name from the Norse 'Thingvollr', the 'field of the thing' or parliament.

A834 west up a charming glen to Strathpeffer (5 miles).

Strathpeffer (many hotels) is a large village and old-established spa in the sheltered and richly-wooded glen. The Spa Pavilion contains a pump room and ballroom. From the golf course, to the north, a wide view opens, dominated by the great mass of Ben Wyvis (3433 feet), rising farther north. On the ridge to the east of the village is the vitrified fort of Knockfarrel, affording another fine view. A Highland Gathering takes place at Strathpeffer in August.

A834 on to Contin (2½ miles; hotels), on the north side of Strath Conon, then A832 (right) through the wooded valley of the Blackwater, passing near the Falls of Rogie, to Loch Garve and thence to Garve (6½ miles more).

Garve (hotels) is a village near the junction of Strath Garve with Strath Bran, up which A832 goes on towards Achnasheen (Tour 6).

A835 right, beyond the village, ascending the steep Strath Garve, with Ben Wyvis rising to the east, to the Altguish Inn (10 miles), near the foot of Loch Glascarnoch.

Loch Glascarnoch is a reservoir 4½ miles long, created by damming the Glascarnoch River, the head reach of the Blackwater, and connected by tunnels with a power-station on Loch Luichart, to the south.

A835 on, through rather desolate country to the watershed (915 feet), then descending across Dirrie More to Braemore Lodge (10½ miles).

Braemore Lodge, at the junction of the road to Gruinard Bay and the Inverewe Gardens (Tour 7), stands among extensive pine forests in the glen of the Abhainn Droma, which comes down from the bleak moorlands of Dirrie More, the 'large oak forest' (now treeless). The Ullapool road descends beside the sheer-sided gorge of Corrieshalloch, a deep chasm eroded from the schist, where a footbridge allows a fine view of the Falls of Measach, some 150 feet high.

A835 on, descending the strath of the Broom, then skirting the east shore of Loch Broom to Ullapool (12 miles).

Ullapool (hotels) is a small town and delightful fishing port and holiday resort, with whitewashed houses and a sheltered harbour, at the foot of Glen Achall on Loch Broom, a long impressive inlet of the sea, favoured for its bathing and boating. In Quay Street is the small Lochbroom Highland Museum, with a local history collection. Cruises are operated round Loch Broom and to the Summer Isles, fertile islands in the broad mouth of the loch.

A835 on to Ardmair (3½ miles), on Loch Kanaird, an arm of Loch Broom, then across Strath Kanaird to Drumrunie Lodge (7 miles).

Strath Kanaird cuts off the peninsula of Coigach, to the west, which culminates in the long ridge of Ben More Coigach (2438 feet). Beyond Drumrunie Lodge a narrow road runs west beside the quiet Loch Lurgainn and under Culbeag (2523 feet) and Stac Pollaidh (Stack Polly; 2009 feet), curious peaks of Torridonian sandstone, to Baddagyle (8½ miles), from which it goes on to round Loch Oscaig to Achiltibuie (6½ miles), facing the Summer Isles on the north side of the large bay that separates Coigach from the entrances to Loch Broom and Little Loch Broom. Another road (narrow, winding and very hilly) runs north from Baddagyle, on the east side of Enard Bay, to Inverkirkaig (9 miles), at the foot of the River Kirkaig in Loch Kirkaig, and thence to Lochinver (3 miles), on Tour 9 (page 54).

A835 on from Drumrunie Lodge, a moorland road across a ridge between Cul Mòr (2786 feet) and the Cromalt Hills, to Elphin (8½ miles), with the double-topped peak of Suilven (2399 feet) to the north-west, and thence to Ledmore (2 miles farther); then A837 right (east) via Strath Oykel to Inveran (26½ miles) and A836 on to Bonar Bridge (4 miles).

Ledmore and the road thence to Bonar Bridge are described in Tour 9 (pages 53-54).

A9 (right), crossing the strath between the Kyle of Sutherland and the Dornoch Firth, then along the south shore of the firth—leaving A836, a shorter but hilly road to Dingwall on the right (often difficult in winter)—to Edderton (10 miles).

Edderton, well situated on Cambuscurrie Bay, an inlet of the Dornoch Firth, has an 18th-century Church with a pleasant interior.

A9 on to Tain (5½ miles).

Tain (hotels) is a delightful small market town and an old royal burgh with a beautiful view across the firth to Dornoch Cathedral. Its name is derived from the Norse 'Thing', or parliament. The dominating Town Hall, in the main street, incorporates a tower of about 1730. To the north of it is the Church of St. Duthus, a fine 14th-century building with interesting details, restored in 1876 as a memorial to Patrick Hamilton, the earliest martyr of the Scottish Reformation, burned in 1528 at St. Andrews for heresy.

Beside the sandy shore is an excellent golf course and in the cemetery between the town and this is a ruined 13th-century Chapel dedicated to the 11th-century St. Duthus or Dubhthaich, bishop of Ross and a native of Tain. James IV made an annual pilgrimage here in 1493-1513 as a penance for his complicity in his father's murder.

A9 on across the fertile Fearn peninsula to Milton (6 miles).

Milton is a village north of the shore of Nigg Bay, which is noted for its broad stretch of sands. Balnagown House, to the north, is a 19th-century Scottish baronial mansion incorporating a 16th-century tower, once a seat of the Earls of Ross. To the south, near the bay, is Tarbat House, rebuilt in the 18th century on the site of a castle of the Earls of Cromartie, who forfeited their title after the Rising of 1745, but regained it in 1861. The main road passes Kilmuir, which has a church with a 17th-century round tower.

A9 on to reach the north shore of the pleasant Cromarty Firth at Invergordon (5½ miles).

Invergordon (hotels) is a seaport and sailing resort, once an important naval base, with a fine harbour and a long, wide main street. The town is extended eastward by the colourful village of Saltburn. The view seaward extends over the broad sands of Nigg Bay to the two Sutors or steep headlands guarding the restricted entrance to the firth, and on the other side of the water is the long ridge of the Black Isle. Highland Games take place at Invergordon on the last Saturday in August.

A9 on by the firth shore to Alness (3½ miles; hotels)—beyond which A836 (see above) comes in on the right—and thence to Evanton (4 miles).

Evanton (hotel) is at the foot of Glen Glass, which descends from Loch Glass (4 miles long), a wild loch below the steep northern flanks of Ben Wyvis. To the west of the village the River Glass penetrates the Black Rock of Novar, a remarkable ravine with walls over 100 feet high, but less than 20 feet wide in places. It can be reached by a footpath from the Loch Glass road. Foulis Castle, among the woods to the right of the main road, farther on, is an old seat of the Munros, rebuilt in the 18th century.

A9 on beside the firth to Dingwall (6½ miles) and thence to Muir of Ord (6 miles); then as in Tour 6 via Beauly to Inverness (15½ miles more).

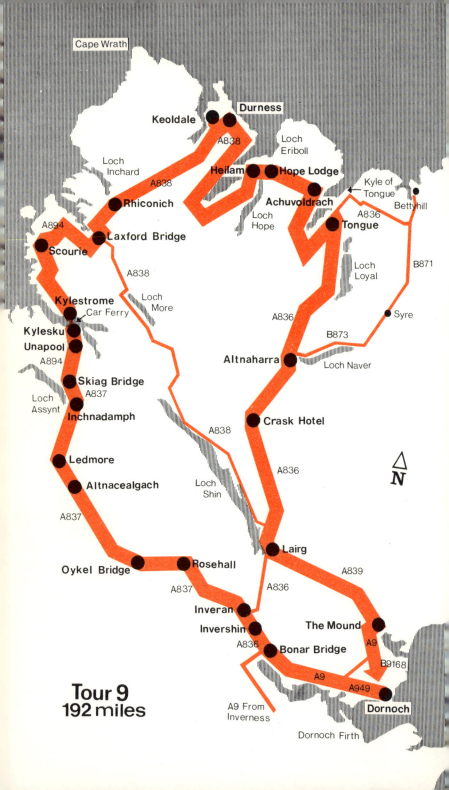

Cape Wrath

Keoldale

Durness

A838

Loch
Eriboll

Loch
Inchard

A838

Heilam

Hope Lodge

Kyle of
Tongue

Rhiconich

Achuvoldrach

Bettyhill

A836

A894

Loch
Hope

Laxford Bridge

Tongue

Scourie

B871

A838

Loch
Loyal

Kylestrome

Car Ferry

Loch
More

B831

Kylesku

Syre

A836

Unapool

A894

B873

Skiag Bridge

Altnaharra

Loch Naver

Loch
Assynt

A837

Inchnadamph

A838

Crask Hotel

Ledmore

A836

Altnacealgach

Loch
Shin

△
N

A837

Lairg

Oykel Bridge

Rosehall

A839

A837

A836

Inveran

The Mound

Invershin

A9

Bonar Bridge

B9168

A836

Tour 9
192 miles

A9

A949

A9 From
Inverness

Dornoch

Dornoch Firth

9. Sutherland and the North-West Highlands

This tour explores much of the county of Sutherland, the extreme north-west corner of Scotland, stretching across country from Dornoch, near the mouth of its Firth, to Cape Wrath. It was named 'south land' by the Norsemen of Caithness (Tour 10), who conquered this region in the 11th century and administered it for about 100 years. Sutherland, though it has some fertile glens, is very sparsely inhabited, partly as a result of the 'Sutherland Clearances' of the early 19th century, when 15,000 crofters were forcibly removed to make way for huge deer forests. Except along the east coast, the county is still today a vast region of empty mountainous moorland with great tracts of heather and bog, and more lochs, large and small, than any other county in Scotland. The tour described below involves the crossing of the **Kylestrome** or **Kylesku Car Ferry**, which normally operates daily and has the advantage of being free, but may be suspended during bad weather. On such occasions the less interesting alternative route from Inveran via Lairg and Loch Shin to Laxford Bridge (see below) can be taken. (Information about the ferry sailings may be obtained by telephoning Kylestrome 202.)

Dornoch (hotels) is a royal burgh and the charming small county town of Sutherland, with pleasant streets and wide squares, an excellent golf course (first mentioned in 1616) and fine bathing beaches, facing the sea to the north of the entrance to the Dornoch Firth. The Cathedral, once the seat of the Bishop of Caithness, was founded in 1224 by St. Gilbert de Moravia (i.e. Moray) and is a building in the early Gothic style. It was damaged in 1570, drastically restored by William Burn in 1837, when the nave was rebuilt and the whole church re-vaulted, and restored again, in better style, in 1924. Of the Castle of the Bishops, destroyed in 1570 by the Master of Caithness, there remains a large tower, which with a modern wing now serves as an hotel.

A949 west for 2 miles, then A9 (left) along the north side of the Dornoch Firth, whose beautifully wooded shores are sheltered by rocky, heather-clad heights, to Bonar Bridge (11 miles more).

Bonar Bridge (hotels) is a small village and angling centre at the head of the firth and on the river connecting it with the wooded glen named the Kyle of Sutherland.

A836 on, through the Kyle, to Invershin (3 miles; hotels) and thence to Inveran (1 mile).

Inveran is at the junction of the Shin with the Oykel at the head of the Kyle of Sutherland. Near the modern Carbisdale Castle, west of Invershin, the Marquess of Montrose made his last stand for Charles II, in 1650. The alternative route to Laxford Bridge (avoiding the Kylestrome Ferry) following A836 at first, ascends the well-wooded glen of the Shin from Inveran to Lairg ($6\frac{1}{2}$ miles), described on page 57. A838, turning left 2 miles north of Lairg, follows the north shore of Loch Shin via Overscaig (14 miles more; hotel), then goes on through wild mountainous country, skirting Loch More and descending the River Laxford to Laxford Bridge (21 miles farther; see below).

A837 on from Inveran, crossing the Shin and ascending the Oykel to Rosehall ($7\frac{1}{2}$ miles).

Rosehall (small hotel) is at the foot of the long Glen Cassley, which descends to join the charmingly wooded glen of the Oykel.

A837 on through Strath Oykel to Oykel Bridge (7 miles) and thence over open moorland, rising above the river, to the Altna-cealgach Hotel ($10\frac{1}{2}$ miles more).

Oykel Bridge is in the centre of angling and deer-stalking country. The road beyond opens up a widespreading view that includes the peaks of Culbeag and Stac Pollaidh (to the west), Cul Mòr, Suilven and Canisp, all heights of Torridonian sandstone standing on a platform of pre-Cambrian gneiss, while to the north rises Ben More Assynt (3273 feet), the highest mountain in Sutherland.

A837 on to Ledmore ($1\frac{1}{2}$ miles), where the road from Ullapool (Tour 8) comes in.

Ledmore stands in a region of barren moorland interspersed with numerous lochs and rivers.

A837 on north, past the small Loch Awe and the limestone crags of Stronchrubie, to Inchnadamph (6 miles; hotel), an angling resort at the east end of Loch Assynt.

Loch Assynt, nearly 7 miles long, is a beautiful inland loch remarkable for the rare plants on its shores and the mountains enclosing it, including the many-peaked Quinag (2653 feet) to the north and the great mass of Ben More Assynt rising to the east. On the north shore of the loch is Ardvreck Castle, a ruined, late-15th-century stronghold of the MacLeods, where the Marquess of Montrose was taken after his defeat near Invershin. From Skiag Bridge (see below), A837 continues round the shore of the loch, with a splendid view of the serrated edge of Quinag, then follows the rushing River Inver to Lochinver ($13\frac{1}{2}$ miles from Inchna-damph; hotel), an attractive fishing village on the small sea-loch of the same name, with a fine view over The Minch to Lewis. B869, a hilly road near the coast, connects Lochinver with Unapool.

A837 on from Inchnadamph, passing Ardvreck Castle, to Skiag Bridge ($2\frac{1}{2}$ miles), then A894 (right), ascending steeply away from Loch Assynt to the pass between Quinag and Glas Bheinn, before descending to Unapool (6 miles more), a hamlet of crofts, and Kylesku ($1\frac{1}{2}$ miles), for the Car Ferry to Kylestrome.

Kylesku (hotel) is on the south side of the narrows, only $\frac{1}{4}$ mile across, which connect Loch a' Chàirn Bhàin or Cairnbawn, on the seaward side, with Loch Glendu and Loch Glencoul, deep fjords running among steep-sided mountains.

A894 on, touching Eddrachillis Bay, with its numerous islets, to Scourie (10½ miles).

Scourie (hotel) is a secluded village and favoured angling resort with a sandy beach on a small bay. From the sheltering heights there are beautiful views over Eddrachillis Bay, to the south, of the isolated Ben More Assynt, Quinag, Suilven and other peaks, and across The Minch to the Island of Lewis. Boat trips are arranged to the island of Handa, with its delightful caves and lofty cliffs, now a sanctuary for sea-birds.

A894 through rugged country with innumerable small lochs to Laxford Bridge (7 miles).

Laxford Bridge, near the mouth of the River Laxford (whose name is Norse for 'salmon river'), is at the north end of the alternative route from Lairg. To the south-east rises Ben Stack (2364 feet), a conical peak of gneiss and quartzite.

A838 (left) through a wild region, with huge masses of gneiss and perched boulders left by retreating glaciers, to Rhiconich (5 miles).

Rhiconich (hotel) is at the head of Loch Inchard, with views of the bulky Arkle and Foinaven to the south-east. B801, north of the loch, descends steeply to Kinlochbervie (4½ miles; hotel), which has been developed recently as a port for herring and white fish.

A838 on over a wide moorland, with good views of the peak of Foinaven (2980 feet), in the great Reay deer forest, then down the broad Strath Dionard to Keoldale (12½ miles; on the left).

Keoldale is on the shallow Kyle of Durness, an inlet of the northern coast which is crossed by a passenger ferry, making it the nearest accessible point for motorists to Cape Wrath, the north-west extremity of Scotland. A minibus, connecting with the ferry, plies in summer to the cape (information may be obtained by telephoning Durness 244 or from the Cape Wrath Hotel at Keoldale). From the beautiful rose-tinted cliffs, which rise to over 500 feet high, or from the lighthouse, built in 1828 (no admission on Sundays), there are wide views over The Minch to the Outer Hebrides.

A838 on from Keoldale to Durness (2 miles).

Durness (hotels) is a village on a bay of the north coast of Sutherland, sheltered by Faraid or Far-Out Head. At Balnakeil, on a bay of pure white sand 1 mile west, is the interesting ruined old church, and in the churchyard here is a monument to Robert Mackay, or Rob Doun (died 1827), the 'Burns of the North'. The 18th-century farmhouse near by is on the site of the summer residence of the Bishops of Caithness and later of the Lords Reay.

To the east of Durness is the Cave of Smoo, a series of huge caverns in the limestone cliffs.

A838 on, passing above the Cave of Smoo, then round Loch Eriboll to its head (13½ miles).

Loch Eriboll is a long, deep and beautiful inlet of the north coast, a safe anchorage enclosed by fine crags.

A838 on round the east side of the loch to Heilam (6 miles), and thence across an isthmus to Hope Lodge (2 miles).

Hope Lodge is finely situated at the foot of the narrow Loch Hope, 6 miles long, above the head of which rises the massive Ben Hope (3042 feet), the most northerly mountain in Scotland reaching over 3,000 feet.

A838 on across the broad moorland of A' Mhòine, with wide sea views, to Achuvoldrach (6½ miles), on the west shore of the Kyle of Tongue.

The Kyle of Tongue is a shallow inlet with white sandy beaches, dominated on the south by the bulky Ben Loyal.

A838 on round the head of the kyle to Tongue (9 miles).

Tongue (hotels) is a pleasant village on a slope above the east side of the Kyle of Tongue. Castle Varrich, on the end of a promontory to the west, was traditionally the seat of the Norse rulers of Sutherland; Tongue House, to the north, was once the home of the Lords Reay, who later controlled all the country hence to the west coast. A836 runs north to Coldbackie (3 miles), with a beach of white sand, then turns inland over the moors to Strathnaver (see below), which it descends to Bettyhill (10½ miles more; hotels), a village finely placed above the estuary of the Naver. It then turns east again, passing the disused 18th-century Farr Church, partly converted into a museum, and the beautiful bay at Armadale, above which there is a distant view of the Orkneys, before reaching Strathy (10 miles; small hotel), from which A836 goes on to Melvich (3 miles), on Tour 10 (page 62).

A836 south from Tongue, ascending with a lovely retrospect of the Kyle of Tongue, then along the west shore of Loch Loyal (8 miles).

Loch Loyal is a delightful inland loch, extended on the north by Loch Craggie (7 miles long in all), and dominated on the west by the soaring mass of Ben Loyal (2504 feet), a granite mountain with great jagged peaks.

A836 on across a barren moorland to Altnaharra (8½ miles).

Altnaharra (hotel) is an angling resort near the west end of Loch Naver, overlooked by Ben Klibreck (2367 feet), a bold mountain of schist rising to the south. B873, skirting the north shore of Loch Naver, goes on to Syre Church (12 miles), where it joins B871 from Kinbrace (Tour 10), descending Strathnaver to Bettyhill.

56

A836 on up Strath Vagastie, west of Ben Klibreck, then over the Pass of Crask, with a fine distant view of Ben More Assynt and other mountains to the west, to the small Crask Hotel (8 miles); then above the bleak Strath Tirry to pass the end of the road along Loch Shin (page 54) before reaching Lairg (13 miles more).

Lairg (hotel) is a favourite angling centre at the foot of Loch Shin, an uninteresting sheet of water 18 miles long, turned into a reservoir to serve a large hydro-electric scheme.

A839 (left), descending Strath Fleet, through moorland country at first, to The Mound ($14\frac{1}{2}$ miles); then A9 (right) for $4\frac{1}{2}$ miles and B9168 (left) to Dornoch (2 miles).

The Mound and the road thence to Dornoch are described in Tour 10 (page 59).

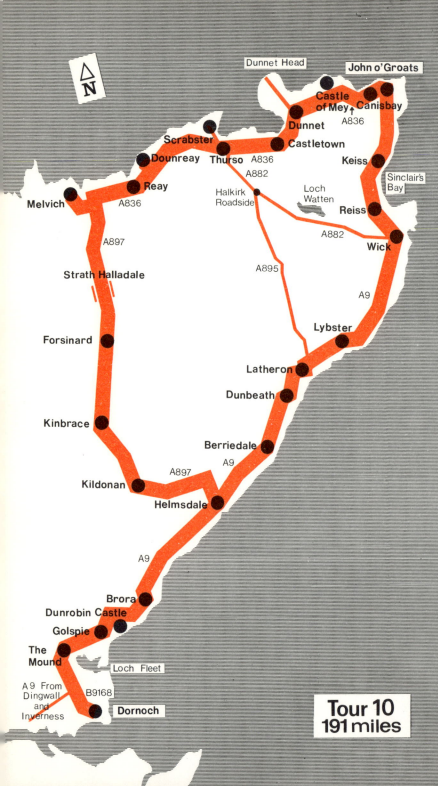

N

Dunnet Head

John o'Groats

Castle
of Mey ↑ Canisbay
A836
Dunnet
Scrabster
Castletown
Dounreay
Thurso   A836
Keiss
A882
Reay
Halkirk   Loch
Roadside   Watten   Sinclair's
Bay
Melvich   A836
Reiss
A897
A882
Wick
Strath Halladale
A895
A9
Forsinard
Lybster
Latheron
Kinbrace
Dunbeath
Berriedale
Kildonan   A897   A9
Helmsdale
A9
Brora
Dunrobin Castle
Golspie
The
Mound
Loch Fleet
A 9 From
Dingwall   B9168
and
Inverness   Dornoch

**Tour 10
191 miles**

10. Caithness and the North-East Coast

This tour, though running partly through Sutherland (see Tour 9), also takes in the smaller Caithness, the northernmost county of the Scottish mainland, with John o' Groats near its extremity. Much of the inland part consists of mountainous and often boggy moorland, but around the rocky coast, and especially in the north-east, there is a considerable amount of very fertile country, and characteristic of this region are the many small, compact farmhouses, some with thatched roofs, and the fields bounded by Caithness flagstones. As in its natural features, so in its customs, Caithness is a 'lowland' rather than a 'highland' county, and very little Gaelic is spoken. It was settled by Norse invaders during the 10th century and there are many survivals of this time both in place names and antiquities, but from the later Middle Ages the county was dominated by the Sinclair family.

Dornoch is described in Tour 9 (page 53).
   B9168 north from the west end of the town for 2 miles, then A9 (right), crossing the River Fleet by The Mound (4½ miles more).

The Mound is an embankment some 1,000 yards long constructed in 1815 by Thomas Telford to reclaim part of Loch Fleet, an almost landlocked inlet of the sea among craggy, heather-clad moorlands. A839 (Tour 9), descending Strath Fleet, comes in on the north side of the river.
   A9 on, returning to the coast at Golspie (4½ miles).

Golspie (hotels) is an attractive village, mainly of one long street of red sandstone houses, with a good sandy beach. In the 18th-century Church are the fine Sutherland loft or gallery and a pulpit of 1738 with a canopy. On Ben Vraggie behind is a colossal statue of the first Duke of Sutherland. Dunrobin Castle (admission weekdays, mid-July to early September, 11 to 6; tea-room), to the east (see below), the historic seat of the Earls and Dukes of Sutherland, on a terrace facing the sea, consists partly of a large square keep with angle turrets. Built in the early 15th century for the 6th Earl of Sutherland, it was enlarged in the 17th-18th centuries and again in 1835-50, in the Scottish baronial style, by Sir Charles Barry, and restored after 1920 by Sir Robert Lorimer. The castle contains fine paintings by Allan Ramsay, Romney, Lawerence and others, and good furniture and tapestries, but is now partly occupied by a boys' school. The formal gardens were modelled in the 19th century on those of Versailles.
   A9 on, passing inland of Dunrobin Castle (1 mile), to Brora (4 miles more).

Brora (hotels) is a village on a bay with a fine sandy beach, at the mouth of the river of the same name, noted for its salmon fishing. On the right of the road 3 miles farther on are the remains of a large Broch, one of the tall round towers, built of undressed stone, mainly occupied during the Early Iron Age and to be found only in Scotland and especially north of the Great Glen.

A9 on, keeping near the coast, to Helmsdale (11½ miles).

Helmsdale (hotels) is a picturesque fishing village in a deep glen with a small harbour, at the mouth of a noted salmon river descending the Strath of Kildonan (page 62). In the now-ruined 15th-century Castle the 11th Earl of Sutherland and his countess were poisoned in 1567 at the instigation of George Sinclair, Earl of Caithness.

A9 on (very hilly, but with magnificent mountain and sea views), traversing the Navidale ravines and entering Caithness near the rocky Ord of Caithness, then by a steep descent to Berriedale (10 miles).

Berriedale is placed among steep hills where two beautiful wooded ravines break down to the shore, with some remains of a 14th-century stronghold of the Earls of Caithness.

A9 on, with Scaraben (2054 feet) rising to the left, to Dunbeath (5½ miles).

Dunbeath (hotel) is a fishing village on a small bay to the south of which, on the cliffs, is the Castle. This has a 15th-century keep, but was enlarged in the Scottish baronial style in about 1870.

A9 on by the cliffs to Latheron (4½ miles).

Latheron (hotel) is another fishing village, along the side of a deep ravine, with an attractive harbour. A road (page 61) cuts across Caithness from here to Thurso.

A9 on to Lybster (3½ miles; hotel), a small fishing port, and thence to Wick (13½ miles more).

Wick (hotels), the county town of Caithness and a royal burgh, is a fishing port, noted for its herring curing. It takes its name from the small bay (the Norse 'vik') on which it stands, with fine cliffs on either side. The harbour was originally designed by Telford, and R. L. Stevenson was employed as an engineer in 1868 by his father on one of the many schemes for its improvement. In the old town, north of the Wick River, are the narrow High Street and the Parish Church of 1830, and in the churchyard is the Sinclair Aisle, restored in 1835, once the burial-place of the Earls of Caithness.

A9 on, rounding the broad Sinclair's Bay, with a splendid sandy bathing beach and many ruined castles above the shore, to Keiss (8 miles; hotel) and then continuing a little inland, passing a lane to the lighthouse at Duncansby Head (see below) before reaching John o' Groats (9 miles more).

John o' Groats (hotels) is a popular tourist resort on the north coast of Caithness, with a rocky and sandy beach, from which there is a magnificent view over the Pentland Firth to the Orkney

Islands. The place is said to be named after John Grot or de Groot, a Dutchman who built a house here in the early 16th century. The John o' Groats House Hotel is the most northerly on the mainland of Scotland. The interesting coast scenery in the neighbourhood of Duncansby Head, the north-east extremity of the Scottish mainland, includes detached rocks or stacks off-shore and deep gashes in the cliffs known as 'goes'.

A9 back for $\frac{1}{2}$ mile, then A836 (right) to Canisbay ($2\frac{1}{2}$ miles more).

Canisbay has a prominent white Church of the 16th-17th centuries (the most northerly on the Scottish mainland) with a restored interior and a tombstone (on the south end) recording the death in 1568 of Donald Grot, son of John Grot. On the right farther on is seen the restored 16th-century Castle of Mey (formerly Barrogill Castle), purchased in 1952 by Queen Elizabeth, the Queen Mother, as her Scottish home (the gardens are open occasionally).

A836 on past the Castle of Mey to Dunnet (9 miles).

Dunnet (hotels) is a village with a good sandy beach on the wide Dunnet Bay. B855 runs north past St. John's Loch to Dunnet Head, a bold promontory that is the northernmost point of the Scottish mainland. The lighthouse here, built in 1832, commands a splendid view across the Pentland Firth to the great cliffs of Hoy, in the Orkneys.

A836 on from Dunnet round the bay to Castletown ($3\frac{1}{2}$ miles), a large village once noted for its flagstones, and thence to Thurso (5 miles more).

Thurso (hotels) named from the Norse 'Thors-aa' ('Thor's river'), is a grey market town finely situated at the mouth of the Thruso River, with narrow streets around the fishing harbour and a promenade facing out across Thurso Bay. It was long the chief port for trade between Scotland and Scandinàvia, and was later known for 'Caithness flags', paving stones made from thin beds of red sandstone, quarried locally. A 'new town' was laid out at the end of the 18th century by Sir John Sinclair, the agriculturalist. Between this and the harbour are the Museum (admission week-days, 10 to 12, 2 to 5 and 6 to 8; closed on Thursdays at 12), con-taining a fine collection of plants and fossils, made by Robert Dick, a local baker, and the ruined Old St. Peter's Church, founded about 1220 by Gilbert, Bishop of Caithness, and partly rebuilt in 1636. Scrabster Pier, 2 miles north-west round the sandy beach, is the starting point for the steamer service to Stromness, on Orkney; and farther on is Holborn Head, with curious chasms and natural arches in the cliffs. A882 runs south from Thurso through level, uninteresting country to Halkirk Roadside ($5\frac{1}{2}$ miles), then turns south-east, passing Loch Watten and following the Wick River to Wick ($15\frac{1}{2}$ miles more), while

A895 goes on from Halkirk Roadside across open moorland country, with a steep descent to Latheron (24 miles from Thurso).

A836 west from Thurso, leaving A882 on the right (for Scrabster; see above), and crossing Scrabster Hill, with a wide view extending from Dunnet Head to the upstanding cliffs of Hoy, for Dounreay (9 miles).

Dounreay, on the cliffs to the right, with a prominent spherical dome, 135 feet in diameter, is an industrial atomic-energy plant begun in 1954 and now being extended.

A836 on to Reay (2 miles).

Reay, from which Lord Reay, chief of the Clan Mackay, takes his title, is a village overlooking the small Sandside Bay. The early 18th-century Church has a belfry with an outside stair and a contemporary pulpit and gallery, or loft.

A836 on, near the coast, with distant views of the Orkneys, re-entering Sutherland before descending into Strath Halladale (5 miles; see below), 1½ miles short of Melvich.

Melvich (hotel) is a village on a slope above the foot of Strath Halladale in Melvich Bay, which is enclosed by fine cliff scenery. A836 (a narrow and winding road) goes on westward to Bettyhill (see Tour 9).

A897 south, ascending the long, green, fertile valley of Strath Halladale, to Forsinard (16 miles from Melvich; hotel), a small angling centre, and then across the barren moors of Achentoul Forest, with the twin peaks of Ben Griam to the west, for Kinbrace (7½ miles more).

Kinbrace is a village of crofts near the upper reach of the Helmsdale River, which flows out of Loch Badanloch, the lowest of a series of connected lochs, in desolate country. B871, passing north of these, goes over from Kinbrace to Syre Church (15½ miles), where it is joined by B873 from Altnaharra (Tour 9) before descending Strathnaver for Bettyhill (12½ miles).

A897 on from Kinbrace, through a district rich in brochs and other early remains, to Kildonan (8½ miles).

Kildonan is a hamlet in the Strath of Kildonan, the narrow glen of the Helmsdale River, a noted fishing stream.

A897 on down the strath, with Beinn Dhorain (2060 feet) rising to the right, to Helmsdale (9 miles; see page 60); then A9 (right) and B9168 to Dornoch (30½ miles more).

Index of Places